Serving the
Building th

Serving the Public – Building the Union

The History of the National Union of Public Employees

Volume One: The Forerunners 1889–1928

Bernard Dix *and* Stephen Williams

LAWRENCE & WISHART
LONDON

Lawrence & Wishart Limited
39 Museum Street
London WC1A 1LQ

First Published 1987
© Bernard Dix and Stephen Williams 1987

This book is sold subject to the condition that it shall not, by way of trade or otherwise, be lent, re-sold, hired out or otherwise circulated without the publisher's prior consent in any form of binding or cover other than that in which it is published and without a similar condition, including this condition, being imposed on the subsequent purchaser.

Photoset in North Wales by
Derek Doyle & Associates, Mold, Clwyd.
Printed and bound in Great Britain at
Oxford University Press, Oxford

Contents

Illustrations

Introduction

When the National Union of Public Employees was established in 1928 it stood firmly on the foundation stones of a history stretching back for almost forty years, but until now there has been no documented account of that history. Because of the fragmented way in which NUPE evolved from a collection of localised and often short-lived organisations there is no single reliable historical account which describes the way in which the union evolved.

In writing this volume we have tried to remedy that deficiency and in the process to give an additional dimension to an important period in working-class history – the period when largely unskilled and unorganised workers began the long struggle to build their own unions and to win the rights of representation and negotiation. By relating the development of trade unionism amongst municipal workers to economic, political and social changes, and the reaction of the working-class movement to those changes, we have endeavoured to show the part that public employees played in the formative years of the British trade union movement.

Readers in Britain of the 1980s, and members of NUPE in particular, will find many similarities between the experiences of the pioneers of public employee trade unionism recorded in this volume and the more recent experiences of the current generation of trade unionists. The campaign against the intrusion of private contractors and the profit motive into the public services was as familiar to trade unionists in the Victorian Britain of the 1880s as it is to trade unionists in the Thatcherite Britain of the 1980s. The same can be said of the related struggle against cuts in public spending: pinch-penny policies leading to a lowering of standards of service to the public and a squeeze on the pay and conditions of the public employee.

Attacks on local democracy are another continuing

experience of municipal workers. Legislative and legal curbs on local councils and councillors who refuse to conform to reactionary policies of central government are a feature of life which has a long history; the experience of the Clay Cross councillors in the 1970s and many others since find an echo in the history of the struggles of the early public employee trade unionists and progressive local representatives. So, too, does the use of the law to impose restrictions on unions in an effort to reduce their effectiveness and thus weaken attempts by public employees to win better wages and conditions. And, related to the struggle of public employees' unions to survive and function in a hostile environment created by a coalition of business interests and right-wing governments, the struggle by unions to establish their right to engage in meaningful political activity is another thread which runs through the early history of municipal workers' trade unionism.

Against such a turbulent background, with so many areas of struggle impinging on the infant unions of public service workers, the historical record of inter-union rivalry and competition – allied to internal dissent and divisions – may appear to strike a discordant note in working-class history during the period covered by this volume. It is true that solidarity has been the positive value in the development of trade unions; but it would be wrong to overlook the fact that in reacting to the pressures of a hostile environment trade unions have sometimes been infected by the negative values of the capitalist society in which they were created. We do not believe it is a function of working-class historians to gloss over or to make retrospective justification of such events in order to present an heroic picture of a purified proletarian past. Rather, we hope that by recording these events we may help towards an understanding of the present which will avoid future repetition.

Similarly, we have found it necessary to record events either never previously published or long since forgotten which expose flaws in the parts played by leading figures in the early history of public employee trade unionism. To gloss over these events in order to eulogise the pioneering leaders would have left unexplained gaps in the development of the forerunners of NUPE. By including them and relating them to the circumstances in which they occurred we hope we have given a realistic picture of all of the difficulties which confronted public employees in their early struggles to build a union.

It must always be remembered that trade unions are not some kind of machine which can be constructed to a precise specification and programmed to respond in a predetermined fashion in a given situation. Unions, by their very nature, are much more like living organisms which embrace a multitude of variables and which respond in a variety of ways to external circumstances. We have tried to present a record of that process as it evolved in the forty years leading up to the formation of the National Union of Public Employees. It is a history of struggles, set-backs and successes which in total stands as a tribute to those thousands of municipal workers who built a union. We must express our thanks as authors to the Executive Council and members of NUPE who made it possible for us to undertake the pleasurable task of writing that history.

Bernard Dix
Stephen Williams

Note on Wages and Prices

In the forty years covered by this volume significant changes occurred in the level of prices and wages making it necessary to provide a brief note of explanation. It should be emphasised that while the methods used for compiling wage statistics had not been standardised in this period, and account needs to be taken of regional variations – especially when dealing with London – the figures do enable worthwhile comparisons to be made. Readers who work at occupations featured in this volume will note that low wages in the public services have a long history and similar effects whether expressed in old-fashioned £sd or their metric equivalent.

The first major survey of wages conducted by the Board of Trade in 1886 revealed an average wage for adult male workers of 24s 7d a week. This was high enough to relegate four out of five of the nation's unskilled municipal workers – sweepers, dustmen, road workers – to below the average. In London many earned considerably less than the 21s defined by social investigator Charles Booth as the bare minimum for existence. In these years low wages meant high infant mortality, chronic under-nourishment, overcrowded housing and the final indignity of a pauper's burial.

Ten years later a Labour Department census found that the average had reached just over 30 shillings, a figure which the municipal employees' trade union had taken as their target since the turn of the century. The Union's 30 shillings minimum was calculated on the basis of the cost of the following necessities of life for a worker and his family in the London area: rent 7s 6d; food and other necessities 14 shillings; coal and light 2s 6d; clothes and boots 3 shillings; additions to and renewal of furniture 2 shillings; sick club payment 1 shilling. At this stage very few municipal workers earned anything like this. The average was 25s 5d in urban districts and 18 shillings in rural areas.

A rise in the cost of living during this period – reducing the real value of the £ from 20 shillings in 1896 to 16s 3d in 1912 – further eroded low-paid workers' wages and provided the basis for the labour unrest which characterised the immediate pre-war years.

The First World War itself brought about an enormous rise in prices forcing trade unions to negotiate improvements in the form of war bonuses which they then attempted to consolidate into the basic wage. Despite this, the real value of many workers' wages was hit by war-time inflation.

Another major census was undertaken in 1924 by the Ministry of Labour which revealed that the 196,000 local government manual workers earned on average 50s 6d at a time when the national average was nearer 60 shillings, in spite of improvements that had been made following the establishment of national negotiations in the early 1920s.

Sums of money are given throughout in £sd, i.e. one shilling = 5p; half a crown = 12.5p; ten shillings = 50p; 30 shillings = £1.50.

1 Private Profit and Public Health

The nineteenth century was an age of radical change in British society, affecting all aspects of economic, social and political life. Manufacturing industry replaced agriculture as the principal economic activity and the factory replaced the farm as the major source of employment. Improved methods of transport and communication drew distant areas into closer contact, and towns and cities grew rapidly, throwing millions of people close together – often in appalling conditions.

These great changes transformed the lives of working people, exposing them to exploitation by employers which was resisted as workers began to form trade unions as protective organisations. The ensuing struggle between workers and employers was at its most acute in the new urban areas. By 1881, nearly 40 per cent of the entire population lived in just six great industrial conurbations: London, South East Lancashire, West Midlands, West Yorkshire, Merseyside and Tyneside.

The concentration of an expanding population in limited geographical areas imposed great strains on the ability of the towns and cities to meet even the most basic needs of the people who were crowded within them. A major source of concern, which reached crisis proportions during the 1840s, was public health. Inadequate drainage and sewage disposal, limited provision of fresh water supplies and overcrowded, low-standard housing combined to create a constant threat to the health of those living in the towns and cities. So acute was the problem that the government conducted a number of enquiries in the 1840s which by highlighting the seriousness of the situation prompted the growth of an influential public health movement whose constant agitation helped to create a wider public awareness of the need for sanitary reform. Consequently new legislation found its way on to the statute-book over the next 30 years; initially this was aimed at encouraging local authorities to provide adequate sanitary facilities but, as time passed and the need for action became more urgent, cajolery was replaced by compulsion and local authorities were placed under increasing legal obligations in the field of public health.

Despite the obvious need for improvements there were many stubborn opponents of any change. Inevitably the slum landlords, who had a vested interest in maintaining profitable urban squalor, were amongst the most vocal of these. But they were not without allies, as was demonstrated in London where the high density of the population had produced the most serious situation. When proposals were made by the government for a single municipal authority responsible for drainage, street cleaning and water supply they were condemned by the parish parliaments – the vestries and paving authorities – and by the formidable Corporation of the City of London on the grounds that the centralising of power was undesirable. The City Corporation covered only six hundred or so acres in the centre of London, but its immense prestige and wealth had enabled it to exercise considerable authority over the whole of the capital for hundreds of years. During the nineteenth century it used that authority to defend the status quo – which meant defending business interests – and to resist successfully any attempt to carry out much needed reform in London local government. As a result London was excluded from the 1835 Municipal Corporations Act – which established new forms of local government structure in the urban areas – and from the provisions of the 1848 Public Health Act, which created a General Board of Health aimed at encouraging improvements in local sanitary arrangements. This resistance to change by the City business interests had disastrous consequences for the people who lived and worked in the fast-growing London area. One historian, Donald Olsen, described the situation as follows:

> London turned from being an object of pride to an object of shame, from a symbol of wealth to a symbol of poverty, from a vision of health to a vision of disease, from one of light to one of darkness.[1]

It was not until 1855 that a measure of improvement began with the establishment of the Metropolitan Board of Works with responsibility for a range of public services on a London-wide basis. But even this was a compromise with the opponents of reform, including the City Corporation and its allies among the more powerful vestries, and as a consequence only partially met the real need for an all-London authority with extensive public health powers.

It was in this haphazard fashion – the product of conflicting interests between the obvious need for the public provision of basic community services and opposition by powerful and deeply entrenched business interests – that the foundations of modern public services were laid. Like much else in Victorian Britain it was the outcome of an uneasy compromise between the class interests of private profit and public demand for urgent positive action.

As the public provision of basic services grew in the second half of the nineteenth century, so too did the number of workers employed in those services; some local authorities employed the workers direct but others contracted the work out to private firms who employed the workers. London, dominated as it was by private business interests, was an outstanding example of the way in which private contractors were employed and, thanks to the work of a social investigator Henry Mayhew in the early 1850s, there are detailed records of the lives of the workers employed by those private contractors. Mayhew's extensive survey, *London Labour and the London Poor*, which was unique in its range and depth of enquiry, examined closely the working lives of dustmen, scavengers and sewer flushers; in the process it provided a cameo of the appalling conditions endured by workers providing essential public services.[2]

In the 1850s nearly all of the dust in London was collected by private contractors acting on behalf of the parochial authorities – the vestries. Initially the contractors paid the vestries for the right to remove the waste and then sold it either to farmers in the countryside surrounding London, who used it as fertilizer, or to brickworks for use in the manufacturing process. For a period the demand for the waste was enormous and the contractors were able to demand high prices and to make correspondingly high profits. But by the time Mayhew made his survey the market situation had reversed; demand for the dust from the farmers and

Nightmen clearing London cesspools, circa 1849

brickworks had fallen so low that instead of selling removal rights, the vestries were forced to pay the private contractors to take the waste away. However, whichever way the market operated, the private contractors were able to maintain a profitable business, but this was always at the expense of their workers and often at the expense of the ratepayers.

Many of the contractors were small firms with only three carts and six or seven men on their payroll but it was the large firms which tended to dominate the market, and to maintain their position they were not beyond resorting to unscrupulous practices. In addition to collaborating in price rings in order to guarantee the highest possible prices from the vestries they also used their dominant position to sub-contract work out to the smaller firms through informal arrangements. When Mayhew tried to find out more about this system he met with resistance, and reported, 'in one yard intimidation was resorted to and the men were threatened with instant dismissal if they gave me any information'. Using such business tactics to fleece the vestries – which meant fleecing the ratepayers – it is not surprising that the contractors flourished. They were, Mayhew reported, 'generally men of considerable wealth'.

That description could not be applied to the 1,800 London dustmen who were employed by the private contractors. They were paid by the load and even when working flat out could not expect to earn much more than ten shillings a week. In the period following 1826 their wages had been cut by half because of the fall in the demand for dust and the contractors' determination to maintain profits by passing the consequences on to the workers in the shape of lower wages. To compensate for the wage cut the contractors expected the workers to make up their money by soliciting tips. This prompted Mayhew to comment, 'the public being thus in a manner compelled to make up the rate of wages which should be paid by the employer'. If, however, the dustmen were too successful in collecting tips the contractors had no scruples about cutting the wage they paid for a load by a proportionate amount. To increase their incomes many dustmen engaged in the Victorian equivalent of moonlighting – they worked as nightmen, clearing the cesspools which still abounded in London.

Seeking to draw a character sketch of the dustmen, Mayhew observed that they were 'mostly tall stalwart fellows' who were great drinkers, some spending half of their wages in pubs where they often had their own dusties' room. In general they were parochial in outlook and only a few could read or write; those who could were 'listened to as oracles, being believed to understand every subject thoroughly'. They had little knowledge of politics and had no trade union or benefit society to protect them.

It was not only the men who were in the dust collecting business. Very often whole families – men, women and children – would work as a team. The men would collect or load the dust, the children would sort rubbish from the dust in the yard and the women would work as what were known as sifters. Mayhew's description of the sifters at work is worth quoting at length because it is a brutal reminder that the loudly-proclaimed Victorian ideals of femininity, gentility and leisure definitely did not extend to working class women:

> They were almost up to their middle in dust, ranged in a semi-circle in front of that part of the heap that was being 'worked': each had before them a small mound of soil which had fallen through her sieve and formed a sort of embankment, behind which she stood. The appearance of the entire group at work was most peculiar. The coarse dirty gowns were turned up behind them, their arms were bared about their elbows, their black bonnets crushed and battered like those of the fish-women; over their gowns they wore a strong leather apron, extending from their necks to the extremities of their petticoats while over this again was another leather apron, shorter, thickly padded and fastened by a stout string or strap round the waist. In the process of their work they pushed the sieve from them and drew it back with apparent violence, striking it against the outer apron with such a force that it produced each time a hollow sound like a blow on a tenor drum. All of the women present were middle-aged, with the exception of one who was very old – 68 years of age she told me – and had been at the business from a girl. She was the daughter of a dustman, and the mother of several young dustmen – sons and grandsons – all at work at the dustyards at the east-end of the metropolis.

Many of the private contractors engaged in dust collection – between 80 and 90 of them – also undertook scavenging, or road sweeping, on a contract basis. The workers employed by the contractors as scavengers – who were an occupational group distinct from the dustmen – worked an average twelve hour day, but in wet weather this would sometimes stretch into fourteen or fifteen hours. The weekly wage of the workers employed by the best paying firms was 16 shillings, but those employed by what were known as the 'rogue' firms received only 14 or 15 shillings. These poorly paying firms, which Mayhew estimated to total two-thirds of the contractors, also frequently forced their scavengers to work longer hours for no extra pay. Such 'driving', as Mayhew called it, was not uncommon in unskilled jobs and where the abundant pool of London's casual labour could be used as a threat by the employers: 'If you won't do the work, there's plenty outside that will'.

Mayhew himself was in no doubt why such conditions existed, he had a clear understanding of what the Victorians called political economy. At its most conservative this recognised the existence of contending classes in society and therefore of antagonism over the distribution of income and wealth. Put simply, this meant that the less an employer paid in wages the more he received in profits. In 1851 Mayhew applied the consequences of this to the system of allowing private contractors to provide public services; and in doing so he advanced arguments which have been echoed by trade unionists on many occasions since then:

> The contract system of work, I find, necessarily tends to this diminution of the men's earnings in a trade. Offer a certain quantity of work to the lowest bidder, and the competition will assuredly be maintained at the operators expense. It is idle to expect that, as a general rule traders will take less than the ordinary rate of profit. Hence he who underbids will usually be found to underpay.

Approximately a third of London's vestries undertook their own scavenging work by direct labour; but conditions amongst these workers were no better than those employed by private contractors because the vestries made widespread use of parish paupers for road sweeping, a practice which Mayhew found more degrading than the use of private contractors. The vestries defended themselves by arguing that by giving jobs to what were described as the 'unemployables' they were getting useful work performed for the parish while at the same time preventing large numbers of paupers from becoming a burden on the Poor Law Guardians and – indirectly – on the ratepayers. They argued that they were therefore performing a philanthropic function and saving money in the process. But, as Mayhew pointed out, the overall effect of this process was to place a further burden on the Poor Law Guardians by forcing out of work those sweepers who would have been paid regular wage rates by the better employers. In the longer term it obviously undermined the general level of wages of the sweepers. But, despite the obvious and blatant exploitation of the sweepers by both the private contractors and the vestries, Mayhew reported that he found no evidence of trade unions – or even hostility towards the employers – amongst the sweepers.

The third group of London public service workers investigated by Mayhew, the sewer flushers, were faced with problems similar to those which confronted the dustmen and the scavengers. And, inevitably, the role of private contractors was evident.

Before the construction of the main drainage system by the Metropolitan Board of Works in the 1860s the condition of London's sewers was nothing short of abysmal. The early nineteenth century sewers had been built to drain only surface water, so as the population grew the pressure on the system increased. But the real problem arose when new sanitary regulations compelled owners to connect the domestic drainage systems of new buildings to the main sewers and not – as previously – to construct cesspools. The consequences were inevitable and horrific: increasing quantities of raw sewage were pumped into the River Thames and its banks were frequently covered with sewage. A public outcry arose which reached its peak in 1848 when it was discovered that cholera was once again advancing towards the capital. Following a report from a Royal Commission a single Metropolitan Commission covering the whole of London was established – replacing the seven separate commissions which had previously existed – and given total responsibility for the capital's drainage system.

Whatever benefits were gained by the creation of the new Metropolitan Commission, an improvement in the pay of sewer flushers was not among them. The new Commission replaced directly-employed labour with private contractors, and Mayhew, writing a few years later in 1851, identified this as a retrograde step responsible for a reduction in wages of the sewer flushers.

In 1848 the wages of sewer flushers had been on a scale from 24 shillings to 27 shillings a week; by 1851 – following the introduction of private contractors – they had fallen to a scale of 21 shillings to 22 shillings. As Mayhew commented:

> It's the old story, I regret to say – a reduction in the wages of the labouring men. But this indeed is the inevitable effect of the contract system.

Not only did the contractors employ men on the lowest possible wages in order to maximise profits, they also forced the workers to spend considerable sums from their wages to supply their own protective clothing and equipment. For example, essential thigh-length wading boots would cost a sewer flusher 30 shillings; three pairs of socks, half a crown; a jacket, seven shillings and sixpence; a smock, half a crown; and a shovel, half a crown. Set against a sewer flusher's wages, these were large sums. As one flusher said sarcastically to Mayhew: 'Ah, Sir, they'll make soldiers find their own regimentals next ...' Mayhew himself noted:

> To contractors the comforts of health of the labouring men must necessarily be a secondary consideration to the realisation of profit. Men can always be found; safe investment cannot.

Given the conditions in which the sewer flushers worked, Mayhew was surprised to find them in apparent good health. Describing them to be 'well conducted men generally', he said that for the most part they were 'fine stalwart good looking specimens of the English labourer'. However, the job was not without its dangers which caused injury and sometimes death. Removing the masses of solid matter that built up in the ducts became particularly hazardous when flushes of water under pressure shot through the system; men were often swept off their feet and carried through the sewers out into the river. One flusher, sitting with his wife, described the work to Mayhew:

> To flush we generally go down and draw the side up and let a flush of water down ... and then we have iron rakes to loosen the stuff. We have got another way we do it as well; one man stands here with a large board and then there's two or three of us on ahead, with shovels loosening the stuff – and then he ups with his board and lets a good heavy flush of water come down. Precious hard work it is, I can assure you. I've had many a wet shirt. We stand up to our fork in the water, right to the top of our jack boots, and sometimes over them. His wife said 'Ah, I think you often get over the top of yours, for you come home here with your stockings wet enough, goodness knows.' The flusher continued 'When there's a good flush of water coming down we are obliged to put our heads fast against the crown of the sewer, and bear upon our shovels so that we may not be carried away and taken bang into the Thames. You see there's nothing for us to lay hold on.

Mayhew's detailed record of the working life of dustmen, sweepers and sewer flushers in Victorian London is unique; there are no such detailed accounts of similar work in other towns so no real comparisons can be made. It can, however, be said that Mayhew, writing in the early 1850s, identified private contract labour – and, indeed, what he termed the 'labour question' in general – as the central problem. In doing so he anticipated by some years the issue that was to provide an important arena of struggle for municipal workers' trade unions and socialist politicians when they began to speak with a loud voice in the late 1880s.

Notes

1. D. Olsen, *The Government of Victorian London*, Cambridge, Mass. and London, 1982, p.11.
2. H. Mayhew, *London Labour and the London Poor*, London, 1968, Volume II, contains Mayhew's description of dustmen, scavengers and sewer flushers, and it is from these sections that quotations are taken.

2 The Growth of New Unionism

Prior to 1855 local government in London was a confused mess of tangled authorities and responsibilities. Not only was there no single authority responsible for the metropolis as a whole but the local units of administration – the vestries, based on parish districts – were often non-functioning and had very little public credibility. Responsibility for local amenities criss-crossed between the vestries, paving trusts and commissioners. In St Pancras, for example, there were no fewer than 19 bodies with jurisdiction over lighting and paving. There was a wide acceptance that London was ripe for reform, but when it eventually came in the form of the 1855 Metropolis Management Act it fell far short of the thorough-going radical measures of centralised responsibilities of the kind advocated by supporters of the public health movement.

The 1855 Act did establish one body – the Metropolitan Board of Works (MBW) – with responsibility for some aspects of administration on a London-wide basis: the construction of an adequate sewage system for the capital and the building of major road thoroughfares. Indirectly elected through the vestries, the MBW achieved success in its early years with the development of a main drainage system which disposed of all London's sewage into the Thames through works at Beckton and Crossness. Situated on the north and south banks of the river on the borders of Essex and Kent respectively, these outfall works were believed to be far enough away from the centre of London to prevent any future health risk to the capital. History subsequently proved this judgement to have been wrong, but at the time of development the system was a marked improvement. Another notable achievement of the MBW was the construction of the Thames Embankment, which was completed in 1870. After this, however, the MBW lost direction and – with no major projects to undertake – it was 'carrying on many of its activities of municipal government but without either the organisation or the power to sustain them'.[1]

The vestries remained intact under the 1855 Act but they were subjected to some measures of reform and rationalisation and they were required to perform their public health functions – scavenging, refuse removal and general cleansing – more efficiently. One important change under the Act was the introduction of a standard system of election to the vestries and a widening of the franchise. Under the new electoral system the electors were required to be ratepayers of at least a year's standing – and, although very limited by present-day standards, the new system did make the vestries much more susceptible to pressure from a population which, through improved educational opportunities, was becoming more aware of public issues. One result of this development was the formation of ratepayers' associations which successfully contested local elections, usually on a single-minded policy of keeping the rates low. Indeed, 'local economy', as it was known, became the watchword for vestries during this period as they attempted to provide the basic services required by law at the lowest possible cost. Commenting on this period, Owen has written:

> to some of them nothing mattered but the rates, and the surest way to get elected was to make resounding attacks on the extravagance of the old members and resounding promises to cut the rates.[2]

This penny-pinching attitude had some unexpected consequences in the provision of services. Often the workers directly employed by the vestries would be very badly paid, but the same vestries would not hesitate to dismiss contractors when they believed the services were overpriced or that the contractors were not providing value for money. Ideological considerations concerning the relative superiority of either direct or contract labour were not an issue; to the vestry members it was simply a matter of what they considered to be 'local economy'. Such was the approach adopted, for example, by the London Vestry of St George's in the East which decided to use direct labour for street cleaning and refuse collection

Clearing the streets, circa 1880

after repeated complaints about the private contractors.[3] Loftier motives sometimes surfaced, as in the London Vestry of Lambeth where the local Medical Officer took the private contractors to task for not collecting frequently enough. An historian of the area remarked:

> The Medical Officer felt that the self interest of the scavenging contractor required that they remove household refuse as infrequently as possible and observed that they were unlikely to make collections from poorer households 'owing to the deficient fees for dustmen which were inevitably there'.[4]

As a result Lambeth, like St George's, turned to directly-employed labour in 1877; a similar pattern was followed in Wandsworth and other nearby vestries.

But the changes flowing from the 1855 Act were insufficient to temper the demands of the critics, and increasing agitation developed for further reform of London local government, which reached a high pitch in the 1880s. Critics such as James Firth, of the London Municipal Reform League, argued that the MBW had failed to provide an effective London-wide administration largely because the 1855 Act did not go far enough in establishing central power in an elected local government body. Firth and his supporters also argued forcibly for the municipalisation of services such as water supply, gas and tramways – pointing to cities like Birmingham, Liverpool and Glasgow where municipal trading was extensive. Implicit in these demands for municipalisation was the belief that the basic utilities were too important to be left in the hands of companies whose main motivation was private profit and not public good. But this argument was not necessarily accompanied by a general critique of the capitalist system; as Lord Rosebery, one of the leading figures in the Municipal Reform League, made clear when he said: 'These things are not socialism at all. They are a vital necessity for a great city.'[5] It was by thus distancing themselves from any notions that such changes were the forerunners of a new socialist society that the advocates of such reforms were able to gather and maintain a broad spectrum of support.

The changes for which the Municipal Reform League

agitated were eventually introduced under the 1888 Local Government Act, which established London as a county in its own right and set up an elected London County Council (LCC) to replace the MBW, which by then had achieved notoriety as well as unpopularity following proof of corruption by its officials. The first elections to the newly created LCC produced a victory for the Progressive Party described by E.J. Hobsbawm as a 'broad liberal coalition of small businessmen and traders, non-conformists and working-class radicals and enemies of the City monopolists'.[6] They defeated the Moderates, who were closely allied to the Conservative Associations. This election result, while originating in nothing more than a reform of London local government, made a significant contribution to an emerging pattern of working-class politics and trade unionism which was to have an impact throughout Britain.

Among the working-class radicals elected to the LCC under the Progressive banner was John Burns. He was one of the many young workers who had joined the Social Democratic Federation during the 1880s as a result of its vigorous agitation on unemployment and free speech which was part of its persistent campaign to popularise the ideas of socialism. Under the idiosyncratic leadership of H.M. Hyndman, the SDF had developed a critique of capitalism based on the Marxist ideas of conflict between the contending classes in society; a conflict which would lead to a revolutionary situation, the overthrowing of capitalism by the working class and the eventual establishment of a classless socialist society. The role that trade unions could play in this process presented a problem for the SDF. Although the unions were clearly working-class organisations based at the points of production in capitalist society, experience supported the theory that unions could have only a limited influence on wages and conditions while the economic structure of capitalism remained intact. The SDF could therefore argue that expensive and ineffective strikes diverted working-class energy and resources away from more fundamental arenas of struggle, such as political agitation and electoral activity. Variations on this position were held at different times throughout the history of the SDF and it sometimes accorded a more positive role to the unions. There remained within the SDF, however, an ambiguity on the question which created a practical problem for its members who were active in the unions – and it was precisely these people who were to provide the leadership to unskilled workers as they began to take up the banner of trade unionism in 1888 and 1889.[7]

The first stirrings of what was to become widespread working-class unrest came in 1888 when match girls employed at the Bryant and May factory in London's East End launched a strike against low pay, authoritarian management and appalling conditions of work. Under the leadership of SDF members Annie Besant and Herbert Burrows, the strikers, a group of the most down-trodden workers in London, scored a widely publicised victory which acted as a catalyst on others. The following summer a fierce struggle by the Gas Workers' and General Labourers' Union – a newly-formed London-based union with SDF member Will Thorne at its head – won a cut of four hours in working time from the capital's private gas companies to establish the symbolic eight hour day. This historic victory was soon followed by a five week strike of London dockworkers which gained wide public support and won the famous dockers' tanner – a pay rate of sixpence an hour – and established a virtual closed shop in the port. The dockworkers were led in their struggle by John Burns, Ben Tillet and Tom Mann – all members of the SDF.

This upsurge of successful trade union activity was of great historic significance. First, it demonstrated that unskilled workers could organise effective trade unions – something which had previously been considered the prerogative of the skilled trades. Second, it showed that militant action could achieve results – such as the eight hour day – that had eluded the skilled workers' unions for many years. Third, the leaders of the New Unions – as they became known – differed fundamentally from the leaders of the old skilled unions. The New Union leaders were predominantly socialist in outlook whereas the leaders of the established skilled unions generally believed that working class interests were best served through the Liberal Party. Finally, in the two years following 1889 trade union membership more than doubled – rising from 679,000 to 1,500,000. The larger part of that growth occurred in industries where the workers were traditionally well organised, but a major boost to trade unionism – in membership and morale – sprang directly from the new energies released by the unskilled workers as they opened up their heroic struggles.

The importance of these factors was apparent to those who were observing the trade union and political scene at the time, including Frederick Engels, who recognised that New Unionism was attempting to redefine the nature of trade unionism. Whereas the unions of skilled workers had been exclusive, conciliatory and their political stance little more than advanced Liberalism, new Unionism had a greater mission. Two of its leading exponents, Tom Mann and Ben Tillett, explained that mission in 1890 when they wrote:

> Poverty in our opinion can be abolished, and we consider it the work of the trade unionist to do this. We want to see the necessary economic knowledge imparted in our labour organisations, so that labour in the future shall not be made the shuttlecock of the political parties. Our trade unions shall be centres of enlightenment and not merely the meeting place for paying contributors and receiving donations.[8]

It was with such enthusiastic optimism that the New Unionists burst on to the trade union scene. Whether they achieved what they set out to accomplish is still a subject of debate and disagreement.[9] What is clear, however, is that the vast agitation built up by the New Unionists created a climate in which what was known as the 'labour question' was placed firmly at the centre of political debate. This was to prove crucial for municipal employees as they began their struggles for improved pay and conditions.

When trade unionism emerged among municipal employees it had the advantage of a fertile soil in which it could take root and grow. Unlike the majority of the unskilled workers who were flooding into the New Unions, municipal workers were generally employed on a permanent or semi-permanent basis which could help provide stability and continuity for the organisations they were to create. Whereas unions founded on the recruitment of casual labour – particularly the dockworkers – experienced violent fluctuations in membership during the first decade or so of their existence, the number of municipal workers in unions steadily increased, reflecting both the growth of this sector of employment and the effectiveness of the municipal workers' unions.

Another ingredient necessary for working-class organisation – a cause for dissatisfaction – was also apparent amongst municipal workers at the time. A survey carried out in 1886 revealed that there had been little improvement in their conditions since Mayhew's study more than 30 years earlier.[10] More than 80 per cent of all road labourers – including sweepers, dustmen and those who made up the roads – and sewer workers in Britain earned less than 25 shillings a week. Workers in London did relatively well, as the survey showed that the further away from the capital one got the lower became the wages. The lowest pay was in the rural areas where, the survey noted, 'rates of wages are largely governed by the rates of wages paid in the same neighbourhood to agricultural labourers'. This arose because elected members of the rural local authorities were often local farmers who had a vested interest in keeping road labourers' wages low in order to retain low wage levels on their own farms. As a consequence the average level of road labourers' wages in rural areas was some 30 per cent lower than in the towns, with the local authorities in the southern counties being amongst the worst employers.

For many years the dissatisfaction amongst municipal workers had been latent, without coherent expression. But the success of the New Unions in organising unskilled workers and winning substantial victories – particularly in London – transformed latent dissatisfaction into positive action by boosting the self-confidence and self-respect of unskilled workers and inspiring many of them to form and join unions. Of course, practical bread-and-butter issues played a large part in winning the massive commitment of unskilled workers to trade unionism during this period. But it would be wrong to underestimate the extent to which a certain idealism contributed to the process. It was an idealism based on the argument that all workers, irrespective of their 'place in society', were entitled to good wages, fair treatment and respect. This growing self-confidence was as significant to the development of consciousness amongst the undervalued municipal workers as it was amongst the dockworkers, who during their strike marched daily through the streets of London in an orderly fashion which demanded respect from the people of London.[11]

The National Union of Gas Workers and General Labourers was the archetypal general union in that it sought to recruit all labourers – in any industry and in any part of the country. This principle had an overtly socialist tone to it as it aimed to establish a union on a class basis and not a craft basis as hitherto. A diversified membership was also a tactical necessity for a militant union like the Gas Workers because it could provide a base for mutual support for separate groups of workers who were in struggle. Thus, for example, if the building labourers were on strike they could be supported by the gas workers and other sections of the union not on strike. Will Thorne and his other socialist colleagues playing a leading role in the Union – including Pete Curran, Karl Marx's daughter Eleanor and her husband Edward Aveling – believed that the general union principle was as relevant for the organisation of workers in the modern industrial capitalist society as had been the earlier unions of skilled workers in the stable mid-Victorian period. And they believed that the craft unions had outlived their usefulness and were being replaced by the revolutionary idea of the general union which had been generated by New Unionism.

Following its success in winning the eight hour day the Gas Workers' Union began recruiting on a wider basis than before, and it seems likely that at this stage they would have approached municipal workers, particularly in East London where the union had established general branches. However, no records exist of any substantial claim or action on behalf of municipal workers by the Gas Workers in the London area and no specific reference is made to municipal workers in the early reports of the Union. This apparent neglect of thousands of potential members in the London area alone was a major oversight by the Union's leadership and by October 1889 a new organisation was beginning to emerge in the London Vestry of Camberwell which would eventually take advantage of the Gas Workers' oversight.

Notes

1. D. Olsen, op. cit., p.193.
2. Ibid., p.219.
3. Ibid., p.316.
4. J. Roebuck, *Urban Development in 19th. Century London*, Chichester, 1979, p.199.
5. Quoted in A. McBriar, *Fabian Socialism and English Politics*, London, 1962, p.195 n.
6. E.J. Hobsbawm (ed.), *Labour's Turning Point, 1880-1900: Extracts from Contemporary Sources*, Hassocks, 1974, p.132.
7. See H. Collins, 'The Marxism of the SDF' in A. Briggs and J. Saville (eds), *Essays in Labour History, 1886-1923*, London, 1971. See also V. Rabinovitch, *British Marxist Socialism*, University of Sussex, 1978, (Ph.D thesis), for an analysis of the SDF's attitude to trade unions.
8. Quoted in D. Kynaston, *King Labour*, London, 1976, p.137.
9. For an introduction to this debate see, J. Lovell, *British Trade Unions*, London, 1977.
10. Return of Rates of Wages paid by the Local Authorities and Private Companies to the Police and to Workpeople employed on the roads, etc., and at Gas and Water Works. Parliamentary Papers 1893 (68).
11. See G. Stedman Jones, *Outcast London*, London, 1971, pp. 315-321.

3 Municipal Workers Organise

With a population of nearly a quarter of a million and stretching across a vast area of south-east London, the parish of St Giles, Camberwell, was the third largest administrative authority in London. Its vestry – like the majority of local authorities in the capital – was dominated by the middle class. Although it employed direct labour for its most important public work, the vestry was not a good employer to approximately 400 manual workers on its payroll. For example, carmen – horse and cart drivers – were expected to work a 65 hour week, including Sundays, in the summer for a pittance wage of 24 shillings. Roadsweepers worked $58\frac{1}{2}$ hours in the summer for the niggardly sum of 19 shillings a week.

The vestry was controlled by the Moderates but amongst the minority of Progressive members were some who had sympathies with organised labour. Among these was William Coote, a stout, bearded compositor in his forties who had been a member of the vestry since the mid 1880s. His commitment to the interests of the vestry workers led to him earning the title 'father of the Vestry Employees Union' after he suggested to the workers that they form a union. Following its establishment he acted as its first secretary for six months.[1]

The initial meeting of the Camberwell workers to form their union, with the title Carmen and Roadmen's Union of the Parish of Camberwell, took place in the first week of October 1889. As can be seen by the title adopted, the workers had only limited ambitions which did not extend beyond their own parochial interests. Coote was elected secretary and the newly-enrolled members drew up their grievances in the form of a memorial (or claim), which was later presented to the vestry by Coote. It is worth quoting this in full because it is not just the first record of a claim submitted by a municipal employees' union – it also illustrates, in its moderate and respectful approach, the lengths to which the union went to reassure the elected members of the vestry that the workers were not a group of conspirators trying to subvert the local vestry.[2]

> We the Carmen and Roadmen in your employ, beg most respectfully to ask you to take into your kind consideration the question of an advance in our present rate of wages.
>
> We are out in all weathers, in the heat and in the cold, and find the sum we receive is not sufficient to provide us and our families with the bare necessities of life, without considering house rent etc.
>
> We find the badges round our legs very irksome, and in some cases they amount to torture, if you could kindly discontinue them in the future, it would be a boon that we should be grateful for.
>
> In addition, Gentlemen, we desire to say that if you could kindly take a liberal view in our case, you will brighten our future in life, and earn yourself the everlasting gratitude of every Carman and Roadman in your employ.[3]

When the memorial was presented to the vestry on 16 October the *South London Observer* reported that the hall was packed with workers waiting to see how their claim would be received. The Moderate members of the vestry questioned Coote on his motives, asking, for example, if he received payment for acting as the union secretary. He responded by defending the union in a conciliatory manner, saying that the requests had nothing to do with 'ultimatums' and did not foreshadow anything in the way of a strike. However, accusations were levelled at him that half of the men had been 'pressed' to sign the memorial. The outcome of the debate was a decision to refer the matter to a special committee of the vestry, which over the next few months considered the union's original application and a series of more specific claims drawn up subsequently and which called for an all-round pay increase of two shillings, the ending of unfair disciplinary treatment by vestry officials and the standardisation of sick pay.[4] The composition of the special committee reflected the Moderate majority in the full vestry and as a consequence its reports did not go far towards meeting the union's claims. Able-bodied sweepers received an extra shilling and were to be distinguished from the second-class sweepers – the old and infirm – who earned 19 shillings; there was a shilling extra for

John Cole, general secretary of the Vestry Employees' Union,
1890-1894

gullymen, but virtually every other group was ignored. The other union claims – relating to the wearing of badges, sick pay and disciplinary procedures – were also rejected.

The small increases – which added only £364 a year to the total wages bill of the vestry – hardly constituted an overwhelming victory for the workers and undoubtedly many of them were disappointed with the result. However, the fact that they had won some concessions – however small – would have been regarded as a most encouraging start and most certainly used by Coote and other activists as evidence of the benefits of trade unionism and collective action.

News of the successful formation of the union in Camberwell spread rapidly to the surrounding parishes and workers in Lambeth, St George the Martyr and Bermondsey joined its ranks and set up their own branches. To reflect this growth the union changed its name, first to the South London Roadmen's and Carmen's Labour Union and then – in an effort to recruit from a wider range of workers – to the South London Vestry Employees' Labour Union.[5] By September 1890 its membership had grown to 600 and it was sufficiently well integrated into the trade union scene to become affiliated to the London Trades Council, which had established itself as the acknowledged parliament of London trade unionism.[6] The union's delegate to the London Trades Council was a young man by the name of John Cole who, following Coote's initial period of office, had emerged to take on the responsibility of secretary. Nothing is known of Cole's background other than the fact that he was an employee of the Camberwell Vestry. For the first few months he worked for the union in a voluntary capacity but, as the membership grew and the job of preparing claims and representing members' interests became more demanding, the need for a full-time secretary became apparent. Cole resigned his job with the vestry and became full-time secretary of the union at a wage of 35 shillings a week working from a small office in Southampton Street, Camberwell.

At this time employers in a number of industries – such as engineering and shipping – launched a major counter-offensive against the new aggressive spirit of the trade unions by combining in employers' associations and using violent strike-breaking tactics. Nothing so dramatic happened in the local authorities, but something of the hardening attitudes to trade unions rubbed off on the surveyors who were employed by the vestries and who – faced with the growing confidence of municipal employees' unions – found themselves in conflict with the workforce. Some of these surveyors were notoriously anti-union and deeply resented the intrusion of an organisation between themselves and the men over whom they previously had complete authority; for although the elected vestry members were formally the employers, in reality the role of the boss fell on the shoulders of the surveyors.[7] This relationship was to present a problem not only to the emerging Vestry Employees' Union – as it soon became popularly known – but to successive generations of municipal employees' organisations. In the 1890s the workers described this authoritarian role of the surveyor as 'tyranny', and they sought to overcome it by establishing the principle that no worker should be dismissed except through an elected committee of the vestry – thereby undermining the autocratic power of the surveyor.

Just how union members were victimised is illustrated by the case of the secretary of the Bermondsey Branch, Henry Hodges, who was dismissed by the superintendent in June 1890; after Cole had taken up the case and the Progressives had forced a debate in the vestry, Hodges was reinstated. The case was remembered with obvious delight by two anonymous correspondents (calling themselves 'Dust and Slop') in a trade union newspaper, *Workman's Times*, two years later. Recalling the fate of the superintendent in Bermondsey they related it to that awaiting other over-zealous officials, particularly in Newington where union officers had been dismissed following 'the action they took in routing the old gang at the Vestry elections'. The two correspondents wrote that it would do the Newington vestry officials good

> ... to go to Bermondsey and see how the thing worked there. Two years ago the Secretary was dismissed twice, and reinstated by the Vestry against the wishes of the Superintendent. Now the table has turned and the Superintendent has gone and the Branch Secretary has taken his place, and the old gang is completely smashed up. So, Officials, please beware.[8]

In Bermondsey the union was fortunate in having a strong

Progressive influence amongst the elected members of the vestry on which it could call for support. In other places, however, the situation was much less favourable and union members were weeded out by surveyors and officials attempting to turn the clock back.[9] But the lesson of Bermondsey was not lost on the union, and it added to the growing conviction amongst active members that municipal workers were in a unique position in that they were able to exert a decisive influence on who their employers were. A policy of winning sympathetic influence on local authorities through the ballot box by securing the election of candidates who were sympathetic to trade unionism was therefore adopted by municipal employees and soon came to be seen as a priority objective in establishing the union. At the same time the militant wing of the labour movement was also realising the general importance of gaining control of the increasingly influential organs of local government.

The ruling Progressive Party on the LCC wasted no time in showing the rest of London that it saw the 'labour question' as an issue of 'supreme importance'.[10] In March 1889 the LCC decided that a fair wages clause be inserted in all contracts with private firms undertaking work for the Council. It was soon realised, however, that contractors were simply ignoring this requirement and as a result John Burns pushed hard to strengthen the clause by proposing a specific schedule of wages which would have to be accepted by firms before they were awarded council contracts. Burns actually wanted to go further and eliminate private contract work completely, but he accepted the wages schedule as a compromise position and it was subsequently adopted by the council in November 1889.[11] In the following year the council declared itself in favour of the principle that workers should have reasonable relief from Sunday labour. In May 1891 the council made substantial improvements for its workers in parks and open spaces: an eight hour day and 48 hour week for winter working and 54 hours in the summer, with a minimum wage of sixpence an hour. More than 300 parks staff were thus the first significant group of LCC employees to receive comprehensive increases, but improvements for other LCC workers were much harder to achieve.[12]

One group which tried without success were employed in

the mental institutions, described at the time as lunatic asylums, which were situated on the outskirts of London to isolate the residents from the general population. The largest groups of employees in these asylums were the attendants and nurses, who were salaried staff and some of whom enjoyed fringe benefits – or 'emoluments' as they were then described – such as board and lodging, laundry and the provision of uniforms. But the basic salary was low and the hours of work were very long, in some cases stretching to 14 hours a day for six days a week. Initially the attendants were deterred from developing a trade union consciousness by what they considered to be their professional status. But by 1890 their reticence began to break down and in November of that year they placed a petition before the LCC Asylums Committee calling for reduced hours for night attendants.[13] The committee failed to act on this request and the discontent this generated amongst the workers channelled them towards trade union activity.

Amongst the unskilled workers, however, the main thrust for trade unionism came from the large number of main-drainage employees which the LCC had inherited from the Metropolitan Board of Works. There were heavy concentrations of these workers at the two principal outfall stations at Beckton and Crossness; there were also more than 100 flushers working in the main intercepting sewers and numerous other smaller groups, such as general labourers and engineers. The conditions under which these men worked were unpleasant, but this was something they accepted in the nature of the job itself. What they were not prepared to accept was a situation where the LCC made a great deal of noise about being a model employer while ignoring the men doing heavy and dangerous work disposing of London's sewage.

The Northern Outfall at Beckton was very close to the principal scene of activity by Will Thorne at the Beckton gas works during the gas workers' strike; it was not surprising, therefore, that a number of the men working at the LCC sewage plant should join the Gas Workers' Union, becoming members of the East Ham Branch. Amongst these was a young man by the name of Albin Taylor, who had been working at the Northern Outfall as an engine labourer since 1889 at a wage of 5 shillings a day.[14]

Born in the small Somerset market town of Castle Cary in 1866, Albin was one of five children of Elizabeth and Edward Taylor – who worked variously as a labourer, flax dresser and starcher in the industries of twine, webbing and sailcloth-making which were based in Castle Cary. At the age of eight, Albin Taylor started work as a half-timer; judging from his above-average reading and writing abilities he must have made good use of his limited school time. At the age of fifteen he ran away from home and began work as a labourer on the Severn Tunnel, which was then under construction. Soon after, in July 1882, he enlisted in the Royal Marines giving a false age of eighteen to improve his reckonable service for a pension and following basic training at Walmer, Kent, he was posted to Egypt in February 1884 as part of the British military force used to supress a national liberation movement there. Taylor was invalided out of the marines in October 1885 with what his papers described as 'heart disease', which meant, incidentally, that he was not entitled to a pension and that his earlier exaggerated concern for the future had been to no avail.

Like many others in the 1880s who were in search of work, Taylor came to London and began work as a labourer with the building contractors Mowlem on the construction of Charing Cross Road. When the firm was awarded a contract at the Beckton Northern Outfall works Taylor went on that job, and when the contract expired he was taken on the LCC permanent staff as an engine labourer.[15] At this time he came under the influence of the Social Democratic Federation and, to use his own words, sat 'expectant – a faithful neophyte' at the feet of the leading socialist propagandists: Hyndman, Burrows and Quelch. The SDF at this time was particularly active amongst the unemployed – of whom there were plenty in the area of Canning Town where Taylor had settled and where there was a small but active SDF branch with Will Thorne as one of its members. In his memoirs, *My Life's Battles*, Thorne looked back on those early days:

At that time we were only about fourteen members, and we held our meetings at the house of one of our members in Lansdowne Rd, Canning Town. A good deal of propaganda work was done in different parts of the Borough of West Ham.

The working class knew little of socialism at the time. They were led by other political parties – and their own ignorance – into being hostile to us, and we met with a great deal of opposition.

Often our opponents attempted violence, and we were told that we were talking a lot of nonsense, and that the idea of socialism and its principles would never be accepted in this country.

Despite this hostility we stuck to our work; we kept up our meetings and we distributed our literature, both at the meetings and at the houses in West Ham.[16]

The first surviving record of Taylor as an SDF member appears in the only minute book of the Canning Town branch now in existence. It records that in January 1890 Taylor was elected assistant secretary and auditor, responsibilities important enough to suggest that he had been a member of the branch for some time and was considered by the other members to have demonstrated his competence to undertake these responsibilities.[17]

The growing dissatisfaction of the main-drainage workers with their situation began to manifest itself in claims for improvements to the LCC Main Drainage Committee, and in October 1889 the Committee was inundated with claims. The stokers at Greenwich complained that they were working many hours of overtime without pay; mechanical engineers protested about long working hours in an unhealthy atmosphere. Many other individual and small group claims were also made; but the most significant and comprehensive was that from the workers at the Beckton Northern Outfall, which demanded a 48 hour basic working week; five shillings a day minimum wage; one week annual holiday; protective clothing – the men were still expected to buy their own boots, stockings and flannels as they had done in the 1850s; and an end to local dismissals. The petition ended with the words, 'unless redress of the grievances be granted on or before 3rd February 1890, the men will refuse to go to work on that date and will remain out until their demands are granted'. In response the Committee singled out the flushers for improvements; conceding an eight hour shift at sevenpence an hour and the provision of protective clothing. In an implication that it was not influenced by threats of strike action, the Committee stated that the improvements had been made 'without reference to the petition'.[18]

Although the claim presented to the LCC Main Drainage Committee did not refer to any specific union the signatories were said to be 'all union men', and the likelihood is that they were members of the Gas Workers' Union at Beckton.[19] However, as a result of its failure to organise the potential membership amongst municipal employees generally, the Gas Workers were beginning to lose members at the outfall works to the Vestry Employees' Union – which was recruiting considerable numbers of LCC employees. In March 1891 Taylor himself showed signs of discontent with the Gas Workers' Union and complained about the amount of money it was spending on administration while the membership was falling. It is certain that in subsequent months his interest and activities focused more on the Vestry Employees' Union as he later admitted that he had been secretary of the Northern Outfall Branch of the Vestry Employees since about October 1891. Taylor's activities with the Vestry Employees' Union created problems with the Gas Workers' Union – of which he was still a member – and allegations that he was 'working against the interests of the union' were raised at a Gas Workers branch meeting in May 1891. As a result Taylor was summoned to a meeting to answer these charges; the general secretary of the Gas Workers, Will Thorne, attended that meeting and he accused Taylor of recruiting members of the Gas Workers' Union at the Northern Outfall into the Vestry Employees' Union. Taylor admitted to being secretary of the Vestry Employees' Union at the Outfall, but refused to resign saying that no substantive charges had been brought against him.[20] He believed that dual membership of the two unions was acceptable, apparently on the basis that the Vestry Employees' Union – unlike the Gas Workers' – was acting effectively on behalf of municipal employees but he still wished to retain membership of Thorne's union because of its wider commitment to socialism. The matter was referred to the Executive Council of the Gas Workers' Union but unfortunately the minutes of that body no longer exist; the probability is, however, that Taylor was expelled because his subsequent trade union activities centred on the Vestry Employees.

Taylor's transfer of allegiance to the Vestry Employees' Union came as it was rapidly outgrowing its original south London base; by the end of 1891 it was able to claim more than 3,000 members, which represented an extremely fast rate of growth even by the standards of New Unionism.[21] By this time the Vestry Employees had members in the majority of London vestries and an emerging organisation amongst LCC and City Corporation workers.[22] The elementary structure which had emerged out of the original development in south London proved inadequate in the light of the union's rapid growth in membership and its expansion over a wider geographical area, so at the Annual General Meeting in March 1891 new rules were drawn up to put the union on a sounder organisational base. The union was renamed as the National Municipal and Incorporated Vestry Employees' Labour Union – although in general it continued to be referred to simply as the Vestry Employees' Union. An Executive Council was constituted which consisted of delegates and leading officers from the branches and supervised the day to day running of the union undertaken by the full-time secretary, John Cole.

The objects of the union were set out in a limited and modest declaration:

> 1. Establish a fund for the protection of members. 2. increase the rate of wages and lessen the hours of labour. 3. reform the system of employment. 4. to pay funeral benefit to members (or wife). 5. to regulate relations between employer and employee.

These objectives, and the way in which they were expressed, were far removed from the class-based approach of the Gas Workers' Union and indicate that the leaders of the Vestry Employees' Union deliberately set out to construct a different kind of organisation from that envisaged by Thorne with the Gas Workers. This intention is illustrated by the very different views adopted by the two unions towards the payment of funeral benefit. Thorne wrote in 1889: 'I do not believe in having sick pay, out of work pay and a number of other pays, we desire to prevent so much sickness and men being out of work.'[23] The £6 benefit paid by the Vestry Employees on the death of a member – or £3 on the death of a members' wife –

was precisely the kind of payment that Thorne believed weakened the fighting spirit of a union and diverted funds which should be spent on organisation and strike pay. Later, under pressure from his districts, Thorne was forced to introduce sickness and funeral benefits; but the Gas Workers' initial hostility to such payments and the willingness of the Vestry Employees to pay a substantial funeral benefit on a low contribution of twopence a week must have been a strong attraction to workers to join the Vestry Employees. This was particularly true because of the widespread fear which still existed amongst workers of the indignity of a pauper burial; a fear played upon by the Vestry Employees' Union rule on funeral benefits which specifically mentioned, 'the object being to avoid the possibility of a member being buried as a pauper by the parish'.

However, despite the importance attached to cash benefits, the main thrust of the Vestry Employees' Union remained clearly directed to winning improvements in the pay and conditions of its members. But in order to make gains for its members employed by local authorities the union also recognised that it would have to take action to limit the use of private contractors, because the low pay and long hours imposed by these contractors presented a constant threat to the union's members by undermining their bargaining position.

NOTES

1. *London. A Journal of Civic and Social Progress.* (Hereafter *London*), 11 May 1893.
2. J. Lovell, in his study, *Stevedores and Dockers*, London, 1969, notes that 'dustmen, slopmen and scavengers' joined the Labour Protection League in the summer of 1872 in the East End of London. p.64. It is unlikely, however, that the League managed to make much of an impact amongst municipal workers and they probably dropped away as the League's influence began to wane in the second half of the 1870s.
3. Camberwell Vestry Minutes, 16 October 1889. The badges referred to in the memorial probably carried the Vestry emblem.
4. *South London Observer*, 19 October 1889. Camberwell Vestry Minutes, 27 November 1889.
5. *Workmans Times* 23 January 1892. London and Suburban Trade Union Guide, London, 1891, p.16.

6. London Trades Council Annual Report, 1890.

7. George Duckworth in his section on 'Municipal Labour' in the Booth study wrote of surveyors 'though they are nominally the servants of the ratepayers, the actual master of the Vestry employees is in every sense the surveyor, who is responsible for the control of all labour employed, and who generally, personally engages all permanent hands'. C. Booth *Life and Labour of the People of London*, London, 1903, Industry Series Vol.4, p.27.
The surveyor to the Hackney Board of Works illustrated his hostility to trade unions when he complained of increasing labour costs which he said was the result of labour unions. 'Workmen are urged to discontent and naturally unite in endeavour to obtain more wages and to work less for the higher pay.' *Local Government Journal*, 30 December 1893.

8. *Workman's Times*, 4 June 1892. In Battersea in 1892, hostility to the union was only thinly veiled when the Vestry refused to admit a union deputation following a dismissal on the grounds that all the members of the deputations were from outside Battersea. Battersea Vestry Minutes, 22 March 1892.

9. Given this, it is perhaps surprising that in his evidence to the Royal Commission on Labour, Cole should say: '... a good deal that has been said about intimidation is more apparent than real, there has been nothing in it. I do not know of a case where the Vestry or the local Board have opposed us'. Royal Commission on Labour. Parliamentary Papers 1893/4 (33).

10. The phrase is that of an LCC member and historian of the first years of progressive rule H. Jephson, *The Making of Modern London*, London, 1910, p.99.

11. K. Brown, *John Burns*, London 1977, p.59.

12. For the details of these see LCC Minutes of the Parks and Open Spaces Committee, 17 April 1891.

13. LCC Asylums Committee Minutes, 18 November 1890.

14. LCC Salaries and Wages Book, January – March 1890.

15. This account of Taylor's early life is based on information obtained from the Somerset County Records Office, his military register of service held at the Public Record Office and an article in *The British Citizen and Empire Worker*, 28 April 1917.

16. W. Thorne, *My Life's Battles*, London 1925, pp.54-55.

17. Canning Town SDF Minute Book, 1890-3.

18. LCC Main Drainage Committee Minutes and Presented Papers, 11 October; 6 December 1889; 17 January; 31 January, 1890.

19. In a letter to Burns, Taylor, along with a number of other Beckton men refer to 'our trade union' (Letter written August 1890). Burns MS Collection, 46289 f. 166.

20. Gas Workers' Union, Canning Town Branch Minute book, 21 March 1891; 8 June 1892.

21. Membership figures are taken from the annual returns published in the Report of the Chief Labour Correspondent of The Board of Trade in Parliamentary Papers.

22. For example, see *The Metropolitan and Provincial Local Government Journal*

(hereafter *The Metropolitan*). 29 November 1890 for a report on the formation of the Kensington Branch.
23. Quoted in G. and E. Radice, *Will Thorne*, London, 1974, p.34.

4 Unions and Local Politics

As the labour question came more and more to the fore in public debate the practices of private contractors undertaking work for public authorities also came under closer scrutiny. There had always been allegations of corruption in the allocation of work to contractors – either on the basis of nepotism or bribery – but now the system of private contracting began to come under attack for perpetuating cheap labour; the allegation being that private contractors were bad employers who encouraged poor workmanship. The antagonism to private contractors transcended political divisions as many Moderates became convinced that direct labour was the best system for work such as scavenging and dust collection; a major influence in developing this political consensus was the London evening newspaper *The Star*. In the run-up to the vestry elections in 1891 the paper echoed Mayhew's comments about the monopolistic practices of the contractors when it wrote:

> The influence of the contractors is still very powerful at vestrydom. Some of the old abuses such as giving contracts to Vestrymen's relatives are stamped out; but there is not fair competition between contractors. The public work given out by vestries is practically in the hands of the monopolists. The contractors combine and arrange who is to have the job as soon as it is advertised.

The newspaper followed this with the accusation that London's streets were the worst kept in the country; it said that people going to work were covered with dust which had remained uncollected from the previous day. Contractors, it alleged, were the guilty party and the immediate remedy was clear – to employ direct labour.[1]

The Vestry Employees' Union and *The Star* did not have to

search very deeply to find evidence against the contractors. In Poplar and Limehouse, for example, the private contractors collecting the dust paid their workers 15 shillings for working six days a week from half-past five in the morning until nine o'clock at night; to supplement these meagre wages the workers were expected to tout for tips, which might amount to a few pence a week. The correspondent who reported these facts in *Justice*, the SDF newspaper, commented that the dockers with their tanner an hour were like aristocrats compared to these men.[2]

The case of the carmen working for private contractors was taken up by the Vestry Employees' general secretary John Cole in his evidence to a Royal Commission on Labour in May 1892. He said that workers employed by the contractors were the worst-paid men in London:

> A contractor works his men – well, they are not really men, they are between men and boys; they come up out of the country and they get them for about 2/6 a day, and of course that enables them to take the contract out at a lower rate than they otherwise could do if they paid proper wages.

Cole also observed that there had been a move away from contractors towards direct labour – a change the union naturally endorsed.[3] An example, among many, where the change to direct labour had been made was at West Ham. Deciding to collect dust with a directly-employed labour force, the borough council stated that the reason for the change from contractors was due to, 'unsatisfactory relations existing between the contractors, the Council and the workmen'.[4] It would be wrong to imply that contractors were swept out of London by the combined force of public opinion, arguments of economic efficiency and trade union agitation; but these influences did have a strong impact on the decision-makers and helped prompt many local authorities to opt for direct labour. It is worthy of note that a change from contract to direct labour inevitably involved a considerable initial outlay on capital equipment; but local authorities were prepared to undertake this because of growing evidence that it was a worthwhile long-term investment.[5]

Alongside its campaign against private contractors the

Vestry Employees' Union – with branches springing up all over London – extended its efforts to win better wages and conditions for its members and Cole was kept busy submitting claims on their behalf. The wealthy vestries in the West End of London were, generally speaking, the worst employers and the most difficult to deal with. Paddington was a particularly bad example, paying its sweepers only 16 shillings a week before January 1890.[6] In sharp contrast many of the vestries in the poorer areas tended to be more generous and one of them, Bermondsey, was considered by the union to be a 'model employer'; certainly it was much more so than the LCC, whatever the public claims of that body. As early as June 1890, Bermondsey agreed to employ only trade union members, and over the next two years its 200 manual workers secured holidays with pay and significant wage increases which guaranteed a minimum of 29 shillings a week for all labourers.[7] When the London Trades Council proposed that local authorities should ballot their workers on the desirability of a 48 hour week, Bermondsey was the only one to do so; not surprisingly, the majority of Bermondsey workers supported the idea!

The difference between Paddington and Bermondsey was, of course, one of political control. In Paddington the Moderates were the dominant force in the vestry and the workers suffered as a consequence. In Bermondsey, on the other hand, the control of the Progressives was continually strengthened throughout the 1890s and this was reflected in its labour policies. Many authorities, however, wavered between the opposing extremes set by Paddington and Bermondsey and these were put under constant pressure by both the Vestry Employees' Union and public opinion which voiced a strong need for local authorities to be 'model employers'. When such vestries received a claim from the union their usual response was to set up a committee to examine the claim and – as there was no agreed rate for unskilled workers as there was for skilled workers – to compare wages with those paid by other authorities. These investigations always demonstrated a wide range of wage rates for the same work amongst different authorities and this led St Lukes, a small vestry north of the City of London, to convene a conference in April 1892 to discuss the establishment of a uniform rate of wages throughout the metropolis. The composition of the conference made it inevitable that no agreement would be reached. On one side were the delegates who supported Bermondsey proposals for a minimum rate of sixpence an hour for unskilled workers and on the other were those, such as Hammersmith, who wanted to pay only two-thirds of that rate to men over the age of 55. In the event nothing was agreed except that skilled workers should be paid the trade union rate – which was already a commonly-accepted practice. When the Bermondsey delegates led by Frank Soutter – a well known London 'labour' advocate – reported back to their vestry it was decided that the St Lukes conference demonstrated the need to organise another, with the workers having direct representation through their union and the London Trades Council.[8] Not surprisingly this second conference, with eighteen trade union delegates out of a total of thirty, supported a scale of wages proposed by the Vestry Employees' Union, with a sixpence minimum rate. The conference called on all London vestries to implement this scale but, predictably, the vestries controlled by the Moderates ignored it.

Through experiences such as the St Lukes conference and similar events, The Vestry Employees' Union grew to know where its friends were on the elected bodies in London, and it worked to ensure that those friends received the support of union members at election times. Conversely, the Moderates and other conservative-inspired organisations made a concerted attack on vestries with pro-union sympathies; these attacks usually took the form of protests that such vestries were extravagant at the expense of the ratepayers. In Bermondsey, for example, the Ratepayers' Association could use as ammunition the fact that improving the pay and conditions of vestry employees and providing casual work for the unemployed had almost trebled the vestry wage bill in three years.[9]

Against this background of growing political awareness the Vestry Employees' Union placed great emphasis on electoral activity and saw the achievement of electoral success as central to the union's work. Municipal employees, it continually argued, were in the fortunate position where they could remove their employers. As Cole said in evidence to the Royal Commission on Labour in 1892:

Our organisation is established on the principle of avoiding
strikes. Although we as an organisation do not believe in strikes,
that is only as it relates to us, because we so shape our course that
we obtain at vestry elections what other organisations have to
provide a strike fund for. We strike through the ballot box.

Cole himself became directly involved in politics soon after he
had resigned from his job with the Camberwell Vestry to take
up full-time work with the union and so became eligible to
stand in vestry elections. He was first publicly mentioned as
a possible contender on the Liberal and Radical slate in May
1891 when *The Star* described him as a 'thorough going all
round performer', who would act as a representative of the
vestry employees of London, and it added that as a former
vestry employee he had 'a first hand knowledge of the working
of vestrydom that few candidates possess'.[10] At an initial
meeting of the ratepayers – where voting was by show of
hands – Cole was elected in second place. Following a call for
the statutory right of a secret ballot he slipped back one place,
but his vote was still good enough to secure his election.[11]

Cole's election was one of the many successes scored by the
Progressives in the 1891 vestry elections, in which they
received strong support of *The Star* with 355 out of the 480
candidates recommended by the paper being elected.
Commenting on the results *The Star* described them as a
'sweeping triumph', and added that work could now begin to
'redeem London local life from the corruption of vestrydom'.
During the run up to the elections the paper had given a clear
indication that it considered the 'shameful treatment' of
London's vestry employees should be a key issue, and it
advised voters to make sure that every candidate was
'questioned on the subject'.[12] This kind of intervention
undoubtedly helped to secure the election of vestrymen
sympathetic to the Vestry Employees' Union, including
Charles Steel who was nominated by the union and secured
election in Bethnal Green even though he did not stand under
the Progressive banner.[13]

Not far from Bethnal Green, however, the political map
took a very different form – and one which caused candidates
to be much more precise in their choice of party labels. The
alliance between advanced Liberals, radicals and working

class socialists which had emerged on the LCC and in many vestries had no place in the politics of West Ham. Following the successes of the Gas Workers and the Dockers in 1889, independent labour politics had emerged strongly in West Ham and the Liberals were bracketed with the Conservatives as enemies of the working class. The SDF exerted a considerable influence on labour politics in the area and when the South West Ham Labour Election Committee was established to secure labour representation on the borough council, the SDF played a leading role. When the Plaistow and Canning Town wards of the council came up for re-election in 1891 the Labour candidates were selected by this committee. Among the list of names put forward by the committee were many prominent labour leaders, including Will Thorne and Gas Workers' organiser Pete Curran. Albin Taylor was also included, and was described by the local newspaper as a 'comparatively unknown man and unskilled labourer'.[14] During the election he proclaimed himself a social democrat – in other words, a member of the SDF – and he told a pre-election rally that if he was elected:

> ... he hoped he would be able to represent them better and in a greater degree than some of those jokers did at the present time. He would oppose pensions for all those who earned more than 50/- ... if they [the labour candidates] get on they would have to go to the [Labour] Committee and report what they have done, and receive instructions from them as to what they should do in the future, and the working men through the Committee would censure a member should he do wrong. The candidates who did wrong should be tightly pledged, and if they did wrong their constituents should order them up to scratch.[15]

Taylor was not elected, he came fourth with a respectable vote of 871 – about a hundred short of being elected. But two Labour candidates did win seats and the break up of the anti-socialist alliance on the West Ham Borough Council began.

One of the new West Ham councillors was Will Thorne, and he subsequently fought tirelessly on behalf of the council employees – this despite the fact that the majority of the unskilled workers were members of the Vestry Employees'

Union rather than Thorne's own organisation. In the seven years following his election, Thorne made 28 attempts to secure better wages and conditions for the council employees but – faced with a Liberal-Tory alliance – he was successful only once. He even spoke at a meeting of the West Ham branch of the Vestry Employees' Union while Taylor was branch secretary, after his apparent expulsion from the Gas Workers.[16]

The Vestry Employees' Union had developed another influential political friend in Will Steadman, who had been elected to the Mile End Vestry in 1890 and to the LCC in 1892. The union centrally contributed to Steadman's 'wages fund' – a method used to provide cash which enabled working men to be elected to public office and to devote their time to the unpaid work involved in that office. The Mile End branch of the union also made a separate donation to this fund and in February 1892 Steadman's opponents on the vestry used this donation to question whether employees of the vestry should be allowed to contribute money to the expenses of an elected member. This move failed when the vestry clerk ruled the matter out of order on the grounds that employees could do what they wanted with their money.[17] For his part, Steadman reciprocated the union's financial support by consistently supporting the employees' cause on both the LCC and the vestry.

The need for 'wages funds' of the kind used to support Steadman generated the demand by trade unionists that payment should be made for work on public bodies; or at least that meetings of those bodies should be held in the evenings, to enable more working people to seek election. Another factor which inhibited trade unionists from securing election to public offices was the anachronistic property qualifications necessary to become a candidate. For London vestries there was a £40 rating qualification – £25 in poorer areas – and this effectively debarred many working people from seeking election. The Vestry Employees' Union voiced the widespread discontent which existed on this matter when its delegate to the 1892 TUC, Con Hurley, moved a successful resolution which called for the abolition of all such property qualifications. In his speech Hurley emphasized the need for the labour movement to intervene in the elections for public bodies which employed large numbers of workers, and he argued: 'A man should have an equal right to sit on these bodies whether he live in a castle or a cabin.'[18]

Greater involvement in local politics and improved organisation enabled the Vestry Employees to issue a detailed programme for the 1893 vestry elections; candidates who declared support for this programme were given in return the support of the union during the election.

The contents of the programme demonstrated that the union was developing a growing concern for a widening range of issues. Prominence was, of course, given to traditional trade union demands: union rates of wages; summer holidays; freedom of employees to combine; the right to appear before a committee of the employing authority before discharge; one week's notice of discharge and the abolition of private contractors. But the programme also included demands which went beyond direct worker-employer relationships: such as the establishment of labour exchanges and municipal workshops financed by local rates; the municipalisation of public utilities such as gas and water; the incorporation of the City of London into the LCC area; the establishment of district councils; and the construction of homes for workers at rents which covered only construction and maintenance costs. Union branches were encouraged to use the programme to intervene in local electoral contests and many did so, some joined Progressive election committees and contributed to election expenses.[19] In vestries where a ruling Progressive majority had failed to meet workers' expectations the elections also gave the union an opportunity to voice its dissatisfaction. One such vestry was Shoreditch where, despite a Progressive majority, the employees were still working between eleven and thirteen hours a day for a wage of between 22 and 25 shillings a week and the vestry had ignored union claims for the abolition of piecework. The Progressive journal *London* displayed the feelings of the union when it asked if the Shoreditch vestry members really were Progressives, and warned them that they would not get the support of the vestry employees if they did not improve their ways.[20]

In formative electoral work of this kind the Vestry Employees' Union followed the same line of activity as its larger and better-known counterparts the Dockers and the Gas Workers – which had both turned increasingly to political activity following defeats in strikes and falling membership – and as a consequence it has rightly been described as being among the pioneers of labour representation.[21]

It was not merely in the extension of its activities over a wider political arena that the Vestry Employees' Union was able to demonstrate a growing confidence. At the union's annual meeting in May 1893 its membership numbered nearly 6,000 organised in 45 branches, and Cole estimated this to be about 60 per cent of all the vestry employees in London. If Cole's estimate was accurate it meant that the union had succeeded in organising one of the highest proportions of potential members among London trade unions; it was certainly one of the ten largest unions in the capital at the time.[22] Members present at the annual meeting were optimistic that the union would be able to extend its recruiting activities outside the London area and thus give effect to their ambitions when in 1891 they had formally added the word 'National' to the union's title; Cole cited the establishment of a branch at Caterham in 1893 as the beginning of this possible expansion.[23] As if to establish a firm base for expansion, the union had established new offices in central London – at 30 Eldon Chambers in Fleet Street.

Reviewing the progress made, Cole said that through good organisation the union had made a 'wonderful change' over the previous three years. Increases in one department or another had been made by almost every authority in London, with something like £30,000 being secured each year without strike action being taken. Cole asserted that relations with the vestries were improving with the 'democratic spirit which is growing', and he expressed great optimism for the future of the union.[24]

Seeking groups of workers where there would be potential members the union identified a number of specific areas. For example, although the municipal workforce was over-whelmingly male, there had been a small growth in the number of women employed by local authorities as public lavatory and swimming bath attendants; recognising the membership potential involved, the 1893 annual meeting called on the union to recruit these women workers. Other groups seen as possible recruits included the London Fire Brigade[25] and the LCC asylum workers – for whom a branch was set up at Hanwell in 1893.[26]

The typical method of recruitment occurred after the union

had submitted a claim on behalf of a group of employees. Frequently the claim would be accompanied by a strongly-worded resolution, drawn up at a meeting of 'ratepayers', calling on the employing authority to pay the workers and to accept trade union rates of wages; other organisations – such as Radical Clubs and SDF branches – would also write to the employing authority, pledging support for the workers. Another popular recruiting method adopted was that of free 'branch nights', where new members were permitted to join without having to pay the usual shilling entrance fee. Once new members had been enrolled the system of using collecting stewards at the pay tables to gather contributions would guarantee that members were regularly reminded of the union's presence.

But, despite its successes, the Vestry Employees' Union still faced a number of formidable problems, amongst which the difficulties presented by bad employers loomed large. Particularly severe were the difficulties created by those vestries which had a built-in majority of Moderate members, and where the union's policy of striking through the ballot box must have had a very hollow ring for the members involved. In many of the London West End vestries there was absolutely no chance of replacing the sitting Moderate members by Progressives, let alone independent labour representatives; and in such vestries the surveyor had almost a free hand in disciplinary matters because he knew that he could count on the support of the elected vestry members in any clash with the union. In the most aristocratic authority – St Georges Hanover Square – workers were liable to fines if they were late or if they smoked; if they swore the surveyor was entitled to withold a day's pay from them.[27]

A special problem for the union was the City of London, where the workers were employed through the City Commissioners – an indirectly elected body which made it impossible for the union to exercise pressure at election times. Consequently, despite the considerable wealth of the City of London and its reputedly good public service, City employees were amongst the worst-paid workers in London. In an effort to overcome this problem the union appealed directly to the public for support. Leaflets were issued entitled 'How the employees of the City of London are sweated', showing how some sweepers were paid only 10 shillings a week and contrasting this with £2,500 spent by the City on a royal wedding gift.[28]

The arrogant attitude adopted by the anti-union vestries was demonstrated in Kensington when – following a claim by the union for a pay increase – one vestryman commented, 'if men could not live on 21/- a week there were thousands outside who could'. After a decision that the vestry would not even consider the claim, another vestryman said:

> These men are receiving additional wages amounting to £2,500, and what are they doing? Why distributing handbills, vilifying the vestry, throwing out inuendoes, and not doing their duty.[29]

For such vestrymen 'doing your duty' was the workers' obligation in what the vestrymen saw as a paternalistic relationship under which the men were looked after by the vestry. To join a union, issue leaflets urging others to do the same and to agitate for better pay and conditions destroyed this relationship. And to the vestrymen it meant that the workers did not deserve their special little treats; like the annual 'beanfeast' or the social and dinner which some vestries provided for their sweepers.[30]

One other problem which began to trouble the Vestry Employees' Union in 1893 did not concern its relationships with employers but had its origins in the rules of the unions: the decision taken two years earlier to introduce substantial funeral benefits for members. Undoubtedly, the introduction of this benefit attracted many older vestry workers to become members of the union because it acted as a kind of insurance policy against the inevitable. But in May 1893 Cole observed that many younger members of the union were dying; of the 31 deaths in the union in the previous twelve months, eight had been aged between 25 and 39. Cole attributed this to the effects of poor living standards and said that but for the union's assistance these men 'in not a few cases would have been buried by the Parish'.[31] In the twelve months prior to May 1894, £200 was paid out in funeral benefits – nearly a tenth of the union's total income from members' contributions. Cole recognised the dangers this presented to the union when he wrote, in a letter to Burns, of the 'great hinderance to our usefulness in funeral benefits. I know we cannot very well alter it at once, but I think in time we can, so that we can have the 2d a week for our own work.'[32] Subsequent events demonstrated that Cole's concern was not misplaced, for the financial problems created by the payment of funeral benefits was to plague the Vestry Employees' Union for the rest of its existence.

NOTES

1. *The Star*, 5 May; 9 May 1891.
2. *Justice*, 19 July 1890.
3. Royal Commission on Labour, op. cit.
4. West Ham Borough Council Minutes, 27 January 1892.
5. The early years of the life of the weekly journal *London* listed regularly those authorities who had begun to use direct labour. See for example, 27 April 1893 for Chelsea; 20 April 1893 for Battersea. In 1891 only four out of thirty-five vestries and district boards surveyed employed contractors for sweeping work. *London Statistics*, Vol. II 1891/2.
6. Paddington Vestry Minutes, 17 July 1891.
7. Bermondsey Vestry Minutes, 16 June 1890; Bermondsey Vestry Annual Report, 1891.
8. St. Lukes Vestry Minutes, 13 April; 4 May 1892; Bermondsey Vestry Minutes, 16 May; 20 June 1892.
9. *London*, 23 February 1893.
10. *The Star*, 5 May 1891.
11. *South London Press*, 6 June 1891.
12. *The Star*, 1 June; 7 May 1891.
13. *Eastern Argus and Borough of Hackney Times*, 23 May 1891.
14. *West Ham and Stratford Express*, 4 November 1891.
15. *Justice*, 7 November 1891.
16. Minute Books of the West Ham Branch of the National Municipal Incorporated Vestry Employees Labour Union, 1892-1899.
17. *London*, 2 March 1893.
18. TUC Annual Report 1892. For the effects of this property qualification in debarring an elected member see, F.W. Soutter, *Recollections of a Labour Pioneer*, London, 1923.
19. *London*, 2 March 1893; Burns MS Coll 46292 p. 161 for St. Pancras activity; *London*, 16 February 1893 for Clapham involvement in local election Committee; *London*, 6 April 1893 for Camberwell branch grants towards progressive election expenses.
20. *London*, 4 May 1893.
21. P. Thompson, *Socialists, Liberals and Labour*, London, 1967, p.102.
22. In an interview with George Duckworth for the Booth survey, Cole admitted that his figure for the total number of vestry employees may have been faulty. He said that Burns put the figure at 15,000 directly

employed and 10,000 indirectly through contractors. Cole said that if there were this many, he couldn't find them. Booth MS Coll., Group B Vol 146.Thompson op. cit., p.54.

23. Booth Coll MS op. cit.

24. *London,* 4 May 1893.

25. The efforts of the Vestry Employees' Union to recruit firemen appear however to have been unsuccessful, although their activity did alarm the Chief Fire Officer of the LCC who in December 1892 reported that 'Labour Unions' were leaving handbills around the stations. He said 'it would be impossible to maintain discipline at all if the men were approached in such a manner, apparently with the approval of some members of the Council'. LCC Fire Brigade Committee Minutes, 15 December 1892. No copy of the handbill referred to survives in the presented papers of the committee, but it seems likely that the 'Labour Unions' mentioned included the Vestry Employees' Union.
Cole spoke at a protest meeting at the Hampstead Fire Station in March 1893. *London,* 23 March 1893.

26. Burns MS Coll., 46292. f 38.

27. *London,* 16 April 1893.

28. Letter by Cole to *The Trade Unionist and Trades Council Record,* 2 January 1892.

29. *London,* 4 May 1893.

30. *The Metropolitan,* 9 January 1892 quotes the Marylebone street sweepers annual dinner at which 200 people sat down to 'an ample supply of beef, mutton, vegetables and plum pudding ad. lib. Tobacco pipes, twenty-seven gallons of ale and thirteen and a half gallons of ginger ale.'

31. *London,* 4 May 1893.

32. Burns MS Coll., 46491 f. 233.

5   The Formation of the MEA

Although the principal strength of the Vestry Employees'
Union was concentrated on workers employed in the vestries it
had also established a base amongst workers employed by the
London County Council and this proved to be of
considerable importance in the subsequent history of trade
union organisation of municipal employees.

In the LCC elections of March 1892 the Progressive Party
secured an increased majority with a programme based on
Sidney Webb's book *The London Programme*, which had been
published in 1891 and used as a source for a series of leaflets by
the Progressives in a campaign leading up to the elections. *The
London Programme* developed much that was implicit in the first
term of the LCC; amongst other things it called for municipal
control of the public utilities, the equalisation of rates and
shorter hours with fair wages for workers throughout the
capital. After the 1892 elections and during the second term of
the council some of these objectives were achieved and
progress made towards others. The first steps towards
extending control of services were taken; the local rating
system was reformed and the conditions of some workers were
improved – notably by the establishment of a Works
Department, which paid union rates, to undertake some of the
building work previously performed by private contractors.
However, the LCC's treatment of its unskilled manual
workers – a pivotal point in labour policy – fell far short of
what was expected by trade unionists and the LCC certainly
did not deserve the label 'model employer' which had been
attached to it by some observers.[1]

As the Vestry Employees' Union extended its organisation
of LCC workers – and there were several LCC branches in
existence by 1892 – demands for better wages and conditions
for unskilled workers increased. In the month following the
1892 election, Cole submitted claims on behalf of workers

employed within the scope of the council committees covering bridges, highways and main drainage. Although the LCC was committed to paying union rates of wages it took the perverse view that unskilled workers had no recognised union rate – this despite the Vestry Employees' Union claim that a 30 shilling minimum was accepted by a growing number of employing authorities as the union rate. Significantly, this was six shillings above the so-called 'moral minimum' rate which the LCC had established in 1892.[2] The LCC ignored the Vestry Employees' claim and established a joint committee to consider, in the words of its chairman, 'the cases of these employees who have no trade unions, and therefore no standard rate of wages'.[3] This amounted to a direct snub to the Vestry Employees' Union and undoubtedly provoked resentment amongst its members.

The LCC committee, however, was dominated by radicals – including Burns and Steadman, long-standing supporters of the Vestry Employees' Union – who could have taken the opportunity to make substantial improvements in the position of the LCC's lowest paid workers. In the event they demonstrated neither the desire nor the determination to do this and shirked the opportunity. When the committee's report was published in March 1893 it completely rejected the call for a reduction in hours and recommended pay increases for only a handful of workers. Sweepers' wages were unchanged at 27 shillings for a 54 hour week. The majority of flushers remained on a wage of 28 shillings and their claim for an eight hour day was rejected because 'their duties although unpleasant, are very light'. The workers at the Northern Outfall had their claims rejected in total.

The minutes of the committee are brief and do not reveal any evidence of detailed debate, dissent or conflict amongst its members. It must therefore be assumed that when they drew up their report the members of the committee had reached agreement on its proposals – or its complete lack of them so far as the workers were concerned. Usually Burns's role was very important in committees of this kind because he made it his business to collect the details of every issue before him and was never reticent in making his views known. On this occasion, therefore, it must be assumed that he made no great effort to influence the committee in favour of the claim from the Vestry Employees' Union. But, as his biographer has written, Burns was 'by no means unthinking or unreasoned in his advocacy of working class interests', and 'like many of the Progressives he had a passion for economy that was to become more marked as the years went by.'[4] This assessment may help to explain why Burns, and his colleagues, rejected the claims of the Vestry Employees' Union when they could have been expected to take a much more sympathetic view.

Burns had been a close associate of the union for many years and its secretary John Cole, along with branch secretaries, frequently used Burns as a short cut when raising grievances with the LCC by writing direct to him at his home instead of to the officer of the council responsible for the appropriate committee. When claims for pay increases were made, Burns would sometimes agree to introduce them to the council in order to add authority to the case.[5] Burns was also frequently invited to be the guest of honour at unveilings of new branch banners, or to be the main speaker at open air meetings. At this time whatever Burns did was newsworthy and even the most innocuous event – such as a tea-social and public meeting to celebrate the third anniversary of the union – attracted publicity when Burns attended.[6] Against such a background, Burns, despite his failure to support the LCC workers in 1893, remained closely associated with the Vestry Employees' Union and continued to take up cases referred to him by Cole.

It was a year after the failure of the union's claim on behalf of LCC workers that Albin Taylor wrote to Burns, on 25 February 1894, seeking advice on an internal matter concerning the Vestry Employees' Union. In this letter, Taylor referred to a 'conference of LCC Asylums and Main Drainage men' which had delegated him and a number of others to seek consultations with Burns and other 'labour men' concerning 'the present distressing circumstances of the above organisation' (the Vestry Employees' Union).[7] For Taylor to approach Burns in such terms indicates that something serious had happened inside the union, but the precise nature of the problem is not immediately apparent. There are no surviving union records relating to this period – only secondary sources such as newspaper reports, diaries and correspondence. But these secondary sources – which

Albin Taylor, a pioneer of municipal workers' trade unionism

otherwise reveal a great deal about the union's organisation and development – are virtually silent on the matter which caused Taylor to seek help from Burns. There are, however, a number of clues which when put together provide a plausible explanation of the problem confronting Taylor and his colleagues.

The most substantial evidence surfaces in 1897, three years after Taylor had written to Burns. John Fitch, who had by then succeeded Cole as general secretary, gave a newspaper interview in which he commented on the favourable position of the union despite the fact that it had suffered 'a serious set back by the defalcations of a former secretary'.[8] This is a strong indication that Cole had misappropriated union funds and had either been sacked by the Executive or had disappeared before he could be apprehended. National and local newspapers reveal nothing of such an event, but this is not surprising because a misdemeanour of this kind would seriously undermine the confidence of union members and as a consequence the senior officers would make efforts to prevent news of it becoming public. Legal records are equally unforthcoming and contain no account of any charges or proceedings against Cole. The records of the Camberwell Vestry, of which Cole had been an elected member since 1891, are also silent, but their very silence appears to contain a clue. In January 1894 – some six weeks before Taylor wrote to Burns about the state of the union – Cole attended what proved to be his last meeting of the Camberwell Vestry and there are no further records of him from that date.

To place this matter in perspective it must be remembered that the embezzlement of funds was not uncommon in the formative years of the trade union movement, and municipal workers' unions would not have been exceptions. With cash contributions of nearly £200 a month being paid into the Fleet Street office of the Vestry Employees' Union, the temptation for people who had never previously handled more than a few pounds, must have been considerable. They could unintentionally slip into a situation where misappropriation of funds became enticingly easy.

Cole's dishonesty – for is must be assumed that is what occurred – began a process of change in the Vestry Employees' Union which, although slow to gain initial impetus, eventually led to major alterations and culminated in the demise of the union. Events in two important areas – in Battersea and in East and West Ham – demonstrate how members responded to this situation and how in doing so they opened up new avenues of development.

One of the earliest branches to be established when the Vestry Employees' Union extended beyond its original Camberwell base was Battersea, a working class district which was the home of John Burns – he became its MP in 1892 – and the centre of a great deal of socialist activity. Following the pattern in most parts of London, the Battersea socialists entered into an alliance with the Liberals and Radicals which controlled the local vestry from 1892 (the borough council after 1900) until the First World War. This Progressive control of the local administration meant, according to the weekly journal *London,* that 'on labour questions the Vestry is fully abreast of the times'.[9] It also eliminated private contractors and built up a direct labour force of 500 workers by 1893. Wages paid by the vestry were better than in most other parts of London and in addition the Battersea workers enjoyed a week's summer holiday with pay and a sick-pay scheme – unusual conditions for manual workers at the time.

In this environment and under the leadership of John Piper and Albert Winfield, the Battersea Branch of the Vestry Employees' Union flourished and by early 1894 it was one of the biggest branches, with more than 200 members. In March 1894, however, the branch broke away from the main union and established itself as an independently-registered trade union under the name of the Battersea Vestry Employees' Labour Union. The rules of the new organisation were almost a carbon copy of those of the Vestry Employees' Union and for all practical purposes it continued to function as it had before, but with the significant difference that it was completely independent. The timing of the breakaway coincided with what Taylor had described to Burns as the 'distressing circumstances' in the Vestry Employees' Union and it is therefore reasonable to assume that the decision of the Battersea branch to secede from the union was the result of Cole's embezzlement. With a strong local union organisation and with a sympathetic vestry as their employers, the

Battersea members must have been confident that they would be better off by freeing themselves from the problems of the Vestry Employees' Union. Their decision was to prove correct because the action of the Battersea workers isolated them from the effects of the disasters which subsequently struck the Vestry Employees' Union.

In another part of London, East and West Ham, another group of workers also took steps to distance themselves from the problems of the Vestry Employees' Union. In June 1892, Albin Taylor had been elected secretary of the local branch of the union in West Ham, where he lived with his wife and two children and where he carried out his political activities. But in October 1893 he resigned from this position, apparently to concentrate his efforts on building the union at his workplace, the Northern Outfall, where he had been promoted to the job of handyman at a wage of 31s 6d a week. At the Northern Outfall there was a group of men keen to promote trade unionism and who were close to Taylor, including two other handymen, John Lazenby and H. Smith. It is probable that discussions in this group led to the decision to hold the conference of LCC workers, mentioned in Taylor's letter to Burns, to consider the crisis caused by Cole's embezzlement. It also appears that the participants at this conference decided to take the first steps to breakaway from the Vestry Employees' Union because a few months later, in April 1894, another meeting was held which brought into existence a new organisation – the LCC Employees' Labour Union. Taylor became the organiser of this new union and William Anderson, a flusher employed in the main sewers, became general secretary. Both were lay offices, but Anderson and Taylor were each entitled to a penny per member per quarter for their work – an indication that both posts were considered to be of equal importance. The apparent arrangement was that Taylor would concentrate on organisational activities while Anderson would undertake the more administrative side of the work – a task which, judging by his fine copperplate letters to the council, he was well-equipped to cope with.

Although it is not known whether Taylor was still active in the SDF at the time of this union breakaway, the preamble written for the rule book of the new organisation was uncompromisingly class-based – a sure sign of SDF influence – and it is more than likely that Taylor had a hand in its drafting. A curious feature of the rule book was that although it was written specifically for LCC employees it could equally have applied to workers in any part of Britain. This is indicated by its opening statement:

> Fellow workers, Trade Unionism has done excellent work in the past, and in it lives the hope of the workers of the future, that is, the trade unionism which clearly recognises that there are only two classes, the producing working class and the possessing master class. The masters have known this for a long time, the workers are beginning to see it [they are] beginning to understand that their only hope lies in themselves and that 'united they stand divided they fall', and that from the master as a class they can expect no help. This is why the LCC Employees Protection Association has been formed: and it embraces every kind of labour and all workers; men and women on an equal footing.

The preamble continued – using the same class-based approach – to promise members that it would help them by raising them from being 'mere beasts of burden', and that it would struggle to make:

> brighter and happier the home of every worker, saving of little children from the hard, degrading, bitter life to which they are condemned today, dividing more equally between men and women the tears and laughter, sorrow and joy, labour and leisure of the world.

It concluded with the strong declaration that the army of labour was marching 'steadily and irresistibly towards its ultimate goal, the emancipation of the working classes'. While such images were common in the socialist movement of the 1890s, it was unusual for them to occupy the first two pages of a trade union rule book. Another unusual feature for a union rule book of the time was the number of specific references it contained to women workers and the need to establish equality between the sexes. One of the specific aims 'to raise wages and obtain the same wages for the same work performed by women as that of men'.

The contributions and benefits of the new union were identical to those of the Vestry Employees' Union and they included the funeral benefit which was causing financial problems for the older organisation. Doubtless the new union considered that any benefits offered to municipal employees by one union must be matched by equal benefits by any competing organisation. But while the new union might have felt that it was necessary to compete in this respect it was also trying to distance itself from the tarnished reputation of the Vestry Employees' Union. This was probably one of the reasons why, when the rules were submitted for official registration, it had been decided to drop the words 'Labour Union' – which were part of the full title of the Vestry Workers' Union – and to adopt the title London County Council Employees' Protection Association (LCCEPA).

The incorporation of the description 'Protection Association' in the title of the new union was of considerable significance because it also indicated the attitude of the founders. Despite the outspoken class-conscious declaration in the preamble to its rule book, the LCCEPA saw its role primarily as a defensive one and did not envisage using aggressive industrial action as an offensive weapon to win improvements in members' wages and conditions. Indeed, it appears that any such action would have been considered a breach of the rules because no dispute benefit could be paid unless the industrial action was in defence of existing conditions. Even within this limitation, strike benefit – 10 shillings for men and 5 shillings for women – could be paid only after the executive had been provided with the opportunity for arbitration and two-thirds of the membership had voted in support of the action through a branch ballot. Clearly, the founders of the new union had brought with them a great deal of the caution of the old and a continued emphasis on using political pressure – rather than industrial action – as the main weapon in the union's armoury. Such a policy also reflected the general response by all union leaders at that time to the limitations imposed on unions by an economic climate that had changed for the worse since the boom days of 1889-91.

The majority of the founder members of the LCCEPA were employed in the main drainage service, but a few asylum employees also became members and these included the first president – J.S. Thomas of Sutton. Members of the Vestry Employees' Union at the Northern Outfall joined the LCCEPA and established one of the first branches of the new union under the secretaryship of John Lazenby; nurses and attendants at Hanwell and Banstead Asylums also set up branches. Growth of the new union was steady, but not spectacular; after twelve months membership had reached 385 – a small but stable base had been established.

One of the early issues raised by the LCEPA was that of working hours; a matter in which the LCC lagged behind many other public authorities, including some controlled by the Moderates. The majority of workers at the Northern Outfall were flushers, earning 30 shillings for a working week of between 54 and 56 hours spread over seven days. In only two London vestries – Stoke Newington and St Marylebone – out of 30 surveyed in 1894 did the flushers work longer hours than those employed by the LCC at the Northern Outfall.[10] The first claim to the LCC for a reduction in hours was made by the Northern Outfall Branch of the LCCEPA early in 1895 when it sought a 48 hour week with no reduction in pay.[11] Characteristically, the claim was shunted off to a joint committee – the device which usually meant that the claim was going to be ignored. But, whatever the intention of the LCC, support for the claim was widespread and this prompted the newspaper *London* – a loyal supporter of the Progressives – to publish an editorial which defended the LCC's labour policy. After stating that it was doubtful if the workers themselves wanted shorter hours the editorial said that instead of agitating against the LCC, 'The London workmen would be wise in their own interest if they help the Council to maintain its labour charter as it is now established instead of seeking better terms.' In fact, the LCC's labour charter applied only to building workers and as such contained no references to either sewer or asylum workers; the introduction of the charter into the debate on the union's claim was therefore very much a red herring. The intention of the newspaper was to make the union feel guilty about making claims for improvements when the LCC was under attack from opponents of its labour policy, and especially its Works Department venture. But this tactic did not convince trade unionists; certainly not a correspondent who signed himself 'An employee at the Barking Outfall' in a sarcastic letter to the newspaper. 'If your article was true in substance and fact,' he wrote, 'the main drainage committee of the LCC has just brought about the millenium of the socialist ideal.'[12]

Relations between the LCC and its workers became even more difficult when the 1895 elections, which were held soon after the LCCEPA had launched its campaign for shorter hours, saw the Progressives and the Moderates win an equal number of seats. Despite this deadlock at the polls, the Progressives continued to have a working majority on the council because they held a greater number of aldermanic seats. However, in such a delicate political situation improvements in workers' conditions were harder for unions to win; and when a scandal erupted about alleged financial irregularities in the LCC Works Department the labour question was relegated to an even lower order on the council's list of priorities.[13] But, even allowing for this, the LCCEPA expected some sort of reply from the LCC – if only a rejection – to its claim for shorter working hours. But there was no response to the original claim of February 1895 and in December of that year Taylor raised the matter with the London Trades Council.[14] He not only reiterated the claim for a 48 hour week for main drainage workers but added a demand for a minimum 60 hour week for asylum workers. The conditions of this latter group had not improved since the early 1890s and – with a basic 14 hour day in a highly stressful environment – they were the most exploited group of LCC employees. Taylor returned to the Trades Council time and time again to get re-affirmation of its support for the LCCEPA claim, and in October 1897 the Trades Council expressed the view that the LCC had treated the union 'discourteously'.[15] In an attempt to break the impasse Taylor even wrote privately to one of the Progressive aldermen suggesting a compromise scheme should the 48 hour claim fail.[16] In the council itself attempts were made during 1896 and 1897 to secure a reduction in hours for asylum employees, particularly by Will Crooks, but each time the proposition was voted down. Union pressure did win some small improvement in 1896 and the LCCEPA subsequently made the most of these by holding recruitment meetings in the area of Hanwell, Claybury and Colney Hatch, where LCC asylums were situated.

In the middle of this campaign for shorter hours a special delegate meeting of the LCCEPA was held and Taylor was appointed general secretary which he combined with his existing role as organiser and received an extra payment of $\frac{1}{2}$d per member per quarter. It is not known why Taylor succeeded Anderson, but he had clearly emerged as the driving force in the organisation and it was a natural development that he should become its senior officer. Anderson remained active in the LCCEPA after he ceased being general secretary, becoming the secretary of a branch based in the Victoria Park area of Hackney.

The LCCEPA's long-outstanding claim for shorter hours was still unresolved when the 1898 LCC elections were held. On this occasion the Progressives regained their original dominance and were returned as the majority party. But, whatever the union may have expected, this electoral victory did not put an end to the problems faced by the LCCEPA in its efforts to establish a constructive relationship with the council. In fact, Taylor complained bitterly that in some of its departments the new council was trying to put the clock back. For example, gas meter testing officers had their dinner break cut by half an hour, their overtime rate abolished and their sick pay cut – conditions which Taylor claimed had not been interfered with for thirty years. The fringe benefits given to asylum workers by the first LCC were also removed, despite union protests.[17]

Adding to the union's problems with the employers were internal difficulties. Taylor complained in his 1897 Annual Report that, despite increased membership, financial strains were having an effect on the organisation; these problems intensified in 1898 when the membership dropped to below the 1895 level. But, despite this, the mood of the LCCEPA leadership was optimistic about the ability of the union to expand and to extend its activities beyond the London area; and in 1899 the name of the union was changed to the National Association of County Authority Employees. It was as a delegate from that organisation that Taylor attended the 1899 TUC and raised the issue of municipal workers' pay and condition on a national level. He successfully proposed a resolution which called for a 48 hour week for sewage workers employed by county authorities as well as parliamentary action to improve asylum employees' conditions, and which urged trade unionists to make the wages of asylum employees an issue with those seeking 'parliamentary and municipal honours'.[18] Having made its debut at the TUC the National Association of County Authority Employees promptly disappeared from the trade union scene when, in November 1899, a delegate meeting decided to change the name of the union once again; this time to the crisper title of the Municipal Employees' Association. By this time the downward slide in membership had been reversed and had climbed to more than 600; it was soon to be boosted by events that were sending convulsions through the old Vestry Employees' Union – which had also changed its name some years before.

Following Cole's embezzlement in 1894, the Vestry Employees' Union had tried hard to pick up the pieces and to continue the good work it had performed in the four years prior to Cole's sudden departure. A new general secretary was installed, John Fitch from Greenwich, who had been 'dismissed from the service of the Greenwich Board [of Works] for agitating'.[19] A new set of rules was drawn up which created the additional posts of organiser and office boy and changed the name of the organisation – which was officially the National Municipal and Incorporated Vestry Employees' Labour Union – to the National Municipal Labour Union. In this way the union set out to give itself a fresh start after a disastrous period in which the convulsions at the top were accompanied by a loss of more than 1,000 members. But, at a time which was tough for all unions, even the depleted membership of the NMLU still gave it a place among the top hundred unions in the country and it was still the leading union for municipal employees, despite the fact that it organised only in the London area.

The local elections of 1894 had again provided the NMLU with an opportunity to show how its policy of 'striking through the ballot box' could be applied; particularly as the abolition of the property qualification and the widening of the franchise had strengthened the union's position by opening up new possibilities for working class representatives. As in previous elections, the union's policies were set out in a programme for endorsement by candidates. This time the programme covered not only the vestry elections but also the contests for the London School Board and the Boards of Guardians; consequently in addition to demands for a 48 hour week with a minimum wage of 30 shillings it called for free secondary schools and the introductions of old age pensions in place of poor relief.[20]

The results of the elections produced an impressive performance by the Progressives, who won control of five vestries – losing only one – and increased their majorities in Bermondsey, Battersea and Shoreditch. There were also personal successes for some NMLU activists; among them Albert James, an LCC flusher and secretary of No.1 LCC branch, who was elected to the Lambeth Vestry, and Bermondsey branch secretary Henry Hodges who was elected to the Bermondsey Board of Guardians which had responsibility for poor relief. In total, the results of the 1894 elections were a significant factor in assisting the NMLU to overcome its internal problems by increasing its ability to win improvement for its members.

The Bermondsey Vestry continued to be the model of a good employer which the NMLU held up as an example to others. Not only did it pay the best wages in London and provide good sick benefits and summer holidays, it also offered positive assistance to the union to organise the workforce. In July 1894 the NMLU local secretary, Henry Hodges, provided the vestry with a list of workers who were not union members and the vestry labour committee decided to instruct these men to join the union and to produce their cards to the committee as evidence that they had done so. The NMLU was also asked to provide the vestry with an up-dated list of lapsed members so that it could be ensured that the Vestry did not employ non-unionists.[21] The close co-operation between the two sides was illustrated further when, in 1896, the vestry decided to generalise a 48 hour working week with the full consultation of the NMLU. Battersea Vestry, which was establishing a reputation as a good employer, also granted a 48 hour week in 1896 after union consultations. Hackney and Islington, where the Progressives had gained control, both faced outstanding and long-overdue improvements, including moves to curtail the abuses of private contractors.[22]

But for every Bermondsey or Battersea there were two or

three vestries which would have nothing to do with unions. The vestries in London's wealthier West End continued to be the worst employers, and Paddington retained its reputation as the very worst employer throughout the 1890s – paying its sweepers only 18 shillings a week during the whole of the decade. Paddington was also very hostile to the NMLU and in 1894 it dismissed the branch secretary, McAuliffe, on charges of idleness and 'dereliction of duty'.[23] A campaign in his defence was mounted by the NMLU and the Paddington Independent and Non-Political League, but the vestry remained adamant that having got rid of a 'troublemaker' it was not going to take him back. One vestryman admitted that 'this man is in an unfortunate position', but added that he was 'in favour of refering him to those Vestry members who had used him for election purposes'.[24] But, despite the decision of the vestry men, McAuliffe was re-instated by the surveyor, who then had to face a vote of censure – subsequently withdrawn – by the vestry for his 'slip-up'.[25] Unfortunately there are no records which explain why the surveyor should have acted in this way.

Other authorities, such as the Whitechapel Board of Works, displayed their antagonism to the union by simply rejecting out of hand any possibility of a union deputation putting the workers' case to the board. Instead it encouraged employees to take their individual grievances straight to board members themselves. Using this procedure, the board argued, 'a better feeling will thereby be encouraged between employers and employed and individual circumstances can be considered'.[26] The real intention of the board was, of course, to establish a way of bypassing the union.

Another problem confronting the NMLU was the system of piece rates, or payment by results, under which workers were not paid an hourly wage but a fixed sum for a given amount of work – which was determined by the employer. The system was most common amongst dustmen and in many vestries it had been inherited from the private contractors who had previously undertaken the work. In 1894 at least six vestries and district boards still paid their dustmen by this method.[27] One of these vestries was Camberwell, which paid the dustmen $7\frac{1}{2}$d per ton of refuse collected. Not all of the money earned was paid to the dustmen; before it was divided amongst the dustmen a supplement was paid to the carmen's low wages and a payment of 4 shillings a day to the trouncers – men who worked on the carts while the dustmen collected. After strenuous efforts the NMLU managed to end this sub-contracting system, when the trouncers were incorporated into the permanent staff in 1896. But the union found it more difficult to end the piece-rate system of payment; which meant that the employers were able to set the pace of work by establishing a low piece rate, forcing the men to maintain high work levels in order to secure a living wage.

The clerk of the Newington Vestry attempted to use piece work to increase the exploitation of loaders in the vestry depot, but his actions were frustrated by a prompt union response. The Progressives had secured control of Newington in 1894 and immediately began to improve the public services provided by the vestry. However, the vestry clerk – a Mr Dunham – aimed to establish his personal authority over the day to day business of the vestry, regardless of who had political control. Usually the vestry surveyor was the most powerful figure in labour matters but in certain areas, including public health, he had to defer to the vestry clerk. It was because of this that Dunham was able, in May 1895, to introduce a piece-rate system for the depot loaders – who shovelled manure and other road sweepings into trucks bound for Kent – under which they were paid a rate of $2\frac{1}{2}$d per ton loaded. Previously the loaders had been paid a daily rate of 4s 6d; this was not a large sum but it proved to be more than the loaders could earn under the new piece rates. The clerk took the decision unilaterally and when a union delegation raised the matter with a sympathetic vestryman it was the first that any elected member of the vestry had heard of the change in the method of payment.[28] When the matter was raised at a vestry meeting the clerk attempted to justify his actions by saying, 'It is a question of whether these men or the Vestry are the masters.'[29] In reality it was the clerk who was the master – or at least he saw himself as such. But by the time this discussion took place at the vestry meeting the loaders had taken matters into their own hands by going on strike.

The loaders were members of the Newington branch of the NMLU, which supported the strike from the start. A collection was organised to raise funds for the strikers and a meeting was held to explain the issues involved to other workers employed by the Newington Vestry. When, a few weeks later, the vestry again discussed the dispute the union organised a lobby of the meeting and the local newspaper reported that the vestry hall was packed with workers; the strangers' gallery was too small to hold the big crowd, which overflowed on to the debating floor. The vestrymen were presented with a report from a committee which had been set up to investigate the matter and this report backed the action of the clerk and said that the loaders should remain on the new piece-rate system. A heated debate followed during which the more advanced Progressive vestrymen condemned piece work as 'slavery', and argued that 'members who were elected on the Progressive ticket [should] stand by the unfortunate men and see that they were not sweated any longer'. When the vote was taken only six hands were raised in support of the committee's report; an amendment was then carried which instructed that the loaders should be returned to the old method of payment – to the accompaniment of 'rapturous cheering' from the gallery.[30] The loaders returned to work, triumphant with their defeat of the clerk's attempt to undermine their conditions. Their jubilation was increased because during the strike they had also stopped strike-breakers who had been brought in from Kent, despite an assurance by the clerk that no outside workers would be recruited to do the loading.[31]

If the Newington workers read the signs, there were important conclusions to be drawn from this strike. First, it had confirmed the value of having as employers elected members who were sympathetic to trade unionism. Second, it demonstrated that even with sympathetic employers the key to success was strong trade union organisation coupled with a willingness to use swift industrial action where this was necessary to resolve a deadlock.

As far as can be ascertained from existing records, the Newington dispute was the only strike of London vestry workers during the 1890s. The NMLU set great store by its arguments that vestry workers did not have to use strike action, but in the case of Newington its executive was forced to support the strike because not to have done so would have opened a rift between the executive and the members who were already on strike.[32] The recourse to swift industrial action was not used again during the lifetime of the NMLU and it appears to have been quickly forgotten by its general secretary, John Fitch. When giving an interview less than two years after the Newington strike he said:

> We are in a singularly fortunate position, in so much as we never need to strike, and indeed, have never done so, for we have it in our power to get rid of our employers at election time.[33]

NOTES

1. For examples of this interpretation see H. Jephson, op. cit. See also 'Trade Unionism Triumphant', in *Reynolds Newspaper*, 26 November 1893. This article suggested that so bold and challenging was the LCC's labour policy that they had 'drawn the sword and thrown away the scabbard'.
2. See Sidney Webb's evidence to the Royal Commission on Labour given in November 1892. Parliamentary Paper 1893/4 (39).
3. LCC Joint Sub-Committee on Wages in Vol 3 of LCC Highway Committee Minutes, 30 November 1892.
4. K. Brown, op.cit., p.60.
5. See *The Metropolitan*, 25 January 1890 for a report of Burns presenting a petition on behalf of the Northern Outfall Employees.
6. Burns MS Coll., 46290 f. 354.
7. Burns MS Coll., 46293 f. 143.
8. *London*, 4 March 1897.
9. *London*, 11 May 1893.
10. Webb Trade Union MS Coll. Group A. Vol XLII.
11. LCC Main Drainage Committee Minutes, 14 February 1895.
12. *London*, 6 February; 13 February 1895.
13. See G. Gibbon and R. Bell, *History of the London County Council*, London, 1939, pp. 235-6.
14. London Trades Council Minutes, 12 December 1895.
15. Ibid., 14 October 1897.
16. Letter from A. Taylor to Alderman Taylor LCC dated 7 November 1897, (GMBATU Archive).
17. LCC Public Control Committee Minutes, 27 January 1899; Letter from A. Taylor to the Asylums Committee dated 9 January 1899.
18. TUC Annual Report, 1899.
19. These are Fitch's own words in an interview published in *London*, 4 March 1897.
20. *London*, 24 May 1894.
21. Bermondsey Vestry Minutes, 16 July 1894; 5 November 1894.
22. For Battersea see *London*, 30 January 1896; for Islington see *London*, 4 April 1894; for Hackney see *London*, 25 May 1895.

23. Paddington Vestry Minutes, 6 November 1894.
24. *Paddington, Kensington and Bayswater Chronicle*, 19 January 1895.
25. Paddington Vestry Minutes, 19 January 1895. See also the attempted victimisation of Frederick Flynn in the Hackney Vestry in 1898. Again after a campaign by the NMLU the Vestry was forced to re-instate him – on a vote of 43 to 42 – and he remained active in municipal trade unionism for many years. See Hackney Vestry Minutes 22 June; 13 July; 12 October 1898.
26. *London*, 8 October 1896.
27. Lists of Wages and Conditions of Vestries in Webb TU MS Coll. Group A. Vol XLII.
28. Newington Vestry Minutes, 29 May 1895.
29. *South London Press*, 1 June 1895.
30. ibid., 15 June 1895.
31. *South London Chronicle*, 15 June 1895.
32. In a letter to the branch secretary in Newington, E.J. Cook, Fitch reprimanded the branch for going ahead with strike action without permission of the EC. Newington Vestry Minutes, 12 June 1895.
33. *London*, 4 March 1897.

6   A Sad Departure

During the 1890s Charles Booth, a social investigator, conducted a survey of poverty in London and published his findings in a multi-volumed work, *Life and Labour of the People in London*. Booth embarked on his survey to disprove the claims, made by socialists like Hyndman, that a quarter of London's population was living in abject poverty. But as his survey unfolded, Booth changed his views and reached the conclusion that socialists were understating the case, and that nearly a third of the people of London were living in poverty.

Booth's survey used sophisticated methods to collect a large quantity of evidence, including a wealth of detail on the conditions of workers employed by London local authorities. The definition of poverty adopted by Booth was a wage not exceeding 21 shillings a week, and even by this very cautious definition there were at least 200 vestry employees living in poverty in 1895 – probably many more as Booth's total number of municipal employees appears to be suspect.[1] The survey recognised, however, that the 21 shilling wage could not be taken as too strict a definition of poverty as many workers had to spend considerable sums of money on items directly connected with their employment, such as travel to and from work, working clothes, tools, etc. Given this, the survey commented 'it is perhaps not surprising if nominal earnings of 25/- to 30/- a week fall within the measure of poverty'.[2] According to this measure, no less than 80 per cent of London vestry employees were living in poverty in 1895. As bad as this was however, it was an improvement on the situation that had existed a few years earlier. Available figures show that in 1891 nearly 60 per cent had lived on wages between 20 and 25 shillings.[3] There had therefore been an overall improvement during the early years of the 1890s, albeit from an abysmally low starting-point.[4]

The survey recognised that these improvements in vestry workers' wages, 'had been affected by the demand that public bodies should be model employers'. It gave street sweepers as an example, describing them as 'socially and financially at the bottom of the scale', although 'the most important class of municipal labour'. In 1886 the street sweepers' average wage was 19s 2d but by 1895 it had risen to between 23 and 25 shillings. At the same time there had been a shift in the policies of local authorities. Instead of employing disabled men – who would otherwise be dependent on the boards of guardians for assistance – the authorities were employing more able-bodied workers as sweepers. One surveyor gave a graphic description of this:

> Formerly this class of work formed a halting stage on the way to the workhouse; men no longer able to work at their regular trades, worn out servants, partially disabled men, partially deaf, failing eyesight, subject to fits, one armed, one legged, men with weak intellect; in fact, social wreckage of every description found a harbour of refuge in this work and kept it as long as possible in order to avoid the house ... All these men have departed from life, and as a result of the higher wages and new rules, brought about by the agitation of the men's leaders, a different class of workman is now engaged.[5]

As the surveyor noted, the NMLU – 'the men's leaders' – had played a central part in raising the pay and status of the sweepers. The pressure of public opinion was also significant; but there is no doubt that without activity by the local branches of the NMLU the improvements, however small, would not have occurred across London on the scale that they did.[6] The union found it harder to make further improvements in wages after the initial gains prior to 1895, but it continued to make significant advances in the form of sick-pay schemes and annual holidays and in 1895 Fitch singled out holidays as one of the most important successes of the union.[7]

The NMLU was slowly recovering from the events of 1894, but by 1897 its membership was still below the level it had been three years earlier. Fitch and his colleagues, however, were confident that the union would grow. They anticipated that the move away from private contracting – particularly for paving and sewer work – would provide new recruits for the union from men who were becoming municipal employees as work was transferred from the contractors. Bermondsey,

Camberwell and St Georges in the East were amongst vestries which established teams of directly-employed paviours and labourers. Many of these had previously been members of the Foot and Carriageway Masons' Society, which gradually declined as direct labour increased and workers became eligible for membership of the NMLU.

In vestries where work was still undertaken by private contractors there were frequent scandals over the allocation of contracts. At St James, Piccadilly, for example, a contract for wood-paving was given to a firm whose tender was £800 higher than any other submitted.[8] A vestryman sponsored by the NMLU, Albert James from Lambeth, made a sharp attack on collusion between Moderate vestrymen and contractors which, he said, demonstrated that the interests of the Moderates were 'neither with the ratepayer or good work, but with that of the contractor or jerrybuilder.'[9] But it was not only the NMLU which condemned the private contractors. In 1897 a prestigious gathering of municipal engineers and vestry surveyors made a strong case for the use of direct labour. The Kensington surveyor told the meeting:

> if there was one description of work which should be undertaken by local authorities it was that of the collection and disposal of house refuse. It was in the interests of the contractors to do as little as possible, and so increase their profits.

Other participants supported the use of direct labour because of the control that could be exercised over the work and the supervision of standards that could be established. Not that there was any shortage of evidence to substantiate the latter point. In the issue of the newspaper reporting the conference there was also a report on the inefficiency of contractors collecting dust in St Marylebone. It said that the contractors had proved expensive, with householders having to pay tips to have the refuse removed, and bins were often uncollected for days, despite letters calling for collection.[10] The same vestry also employed contractors who, a few months earlier, had been fined for failing to remove slops from the streets.[11]

Authorities who employed direct labour were aware that, although their opposition to private contractors was winning public support, there were people waiting for municipal enterprise to make mistakes in order to further their campaign against direct labour – as the attacks on the LCC Works Department had demonstrated. The direct labour authorities therefore made frequent calls to their employees for high standards of workmanship and demanded a strong sense of municipal duty to help prove the superiority of direct labour. An example of this was the appeal made to LCC employees by Sir John Hutton, chairman of the council, in his address of 1894. He said:

> Workmen may not be disposed to do as good work for the Council as for the contractor. Now if this is so, it is little short of suicide on the part of the workman ... I have yet to learn that the British workman will allow the grandest chance that labour has ever had in London to slip through its fingers.[12]

A similar plea was made by the Battersea Progressives in 1896, to which they added an argument on the need for trade unions to defend labour interests, even when employers were sympathetic to workers:

> When any public body gives its workmen the best possible conditions of labour they have a right to expect that services rendered will be equal to that done under a private employer, and any man who shirks or neglects his duty in this respect should be treated by his fellow workers as the enemy, as action of this kind if persisted would eventually destroy public employment with all its advantages. There are many men who think they have secured what they think is permanent employment under public bodies at once cease to pay their trade union, under the impression that they are alright and do not need the union to protect them. This action is as foolish as it is selfish. Grievances are sure to occur even under progressive bodies, and such grievances will be found much easier to remove when the employees have a strong trade union at their back and can act collectively instead of individually.[13]

The 1890s were the decade in which the most decisive battles took place between direct labour and private contracting and by the turn of the century the majority of London authorities employed direct labour forces for the essential public health services, such as street sweeping, drainage and refuse collection.[14] A consensus had emerged which accepted that these services were too important to be the subject of competition between rival private firms whose primary objectives were private profit rather than public welfare.[15] The characteristics which were to distinguish the twentieth century style of local government were beginning to form; the trade union and labour movement played a key role in this process, with the NMLU making an important contribution.

Alongside the gains it made in negotiations with employers, the NMLU continued to enjoy returns for its persistent electoral activity. The West Ham branch reaped the harvest for years of hard work in local election committees when in 1898 a socialist majority took control of the borough council. The benefits for the workers were considerable; over the next five years the council introduced an eight hour day, two weeks' annual holiday, a closed shop and raised wages to the level of recognised rates – which in some cases gave workers a 20 per cent increase. It was also not unknown for West Ham to dismiss council officers following complaints against them by the unions.[16]

In 1896 the NMLU general secretary John Fitch was elected to the Greenwich Vestry and then – as a result of an indirect election – to the Greenwich Board of Works, the body which he claimed had dismissed him some years earlier. Albert James continued to be elected to the Lambeth Vestry until 1900, when ill health forced his retirement. A newly-formed branch at Wimbledon scored an immediate election success when its president, John Penny, topped the poll in the district council elections. Last, but not least, William Everitt – a Progressive vestryman in the very non-progressive vestry of St Georges, Hanover Square – moved close to the union after he had come face to face with the poor conditions of vestry workers. His commitment to the NMLU became so strong that in 1899 he was elected as its treasurer, bringing with him the considerable financial experience he had gained as the owner of several coffee houses in London.

But by the time Everitt took over the books the NMLU was in deep financial trouble, and had been so for at least eighteen months. The fears expressed by Cole in 1893 were being confirmed; funeral benefits were crippling the union's finances and with membership no longer growing disaster was inevitable unless swift and effective action was taken. From the relatively strong position of 1893, when membership had been increasing and a healthy balance accumulating in the bank, the NMLU slid to an approximate break-even point by 1895. From that year on expenditure always exceeded income and the union was forced to draw on its reserve fund to pay its way. The two principal items of expenditure were working expenses – which included full-time salaries – and funeral benefits, with the latter accounting for a third of all money spent. In the December 1898 Quarterly Report to branches, Fitch alerted members to the developing crisis:

> The great strain upon our funds by funeral claims makes it very imperative that something be done by age limit, increasing the contributions or reducing the allowance, if we are to pay our way and hold our own in the movement ... There are doubtless numbers of our members who never think that it takes 720 twopences to pay a member's funeral benefit claim; and that it takes a member 14 years to pay £6 at 2d a week.

In the next Quarterly Report, Fitch appealed to members not to recruit new members who were suspected of being in a 'serious state of health', as many of the recent claims for benefit had been from members with little more than the six months' qualifying membership. The Rules Committee was asked to examine the possibility of increasing contributions or imposing an age limit on members entitled to benefit. But no immediate steps were taken to alleviate the situation despite repeated calls for action.

Debts continued to grow and fears increased that the union was close to financial collapse. Then, in August 1899, a mortal blow was struck when a special enquiry committee discovered that the receipts issued by Fitch showed a deficiency of more than £300. Fitch was immediately dismissed from office and a summons was taken out against him in the City Courts; he was tried in September and pleaded guilty to being unable to account for the money. Admitting that he had fallen into careless ways, he said his 'downfall was due to drink'. In his defence he said, 'we did not understand book-keeping', and he claimed that the financial situation was due to all of the NMLU officials – and not just to him. Money, he said, was

National Municipal Labour Union.

BALANCE SHEET,
Report & Funeral Claims,
To December 30th, 1899. (4 Months)

DEAR SIR AND BRO.,

Herewith is Balance Sheet for the Four Months ending December, 1899

I regret very much that we are not enabled to shew a larger balance in the Bank, but you no doubt remember the position of the Union before I was elected Secretary of the Union, I can only say that I hope the next Balance Sheet will be one worthy of keeping. You will notice that we have made **85 new Members** during the time, which in face of the heavy blow we received in August is not bad.

You will also notice the Funeral Claims have been very heavy, (**£224** having been paid, a sum equal to **1s. 3d. per Member for Funeral Claims during the 4 Months**) (see last page) in fact so large that the Executive Council thought it most important to issue an appeal for a Levy, which I am sorry to say has not been responded to as expected.

An Organizer has been appointed. We have now **3635** Members in the Union, I trust that with his efforts and the cordial co-operation of the Executive and the Branch Officials, we shall be enabled to greatly increase our Membership.

I earnestly appeal to all Members to ask their fellow Workers who are not Members, to join. UNION IS STRENGTH.

Yours fraternally,

Eldon Chambers,
30, Fleet Street, E.C.

H. A. DAY,
General Secretary.

THE GENERAL COUNCIL MEETING
Will be held at the
RED LION, RED LION COURT, FLEET STREET,
On FRIDAY, MARCH 16th, at 8 o'clock.

NMLU notice to members at a time of financial crisis

regularly paid into the bank without going first to the treasurer, as per rule; as a consequence he could not account for the missing funds. He was fined £5 and ordered to pay back the £300 to the union or to go to prison for two months with hard labour.[17]

Fitch was succeeded as general secretary by Herbert Day, a young man who had entered the union's service as an office boy in 1893. He became general secretary automatically when Fitch was dismissed as he had been promoted as assistant to Fitch in 1897, despite being only eighteen years old at the time. Although he had probably acquired considerable administrative skills during his six years with the NMLU, Day's experience of the broad spectrum of trade unionism was extremely limited; to expect him to take over the leadership of a union that was in severe crisis was unfair to both him and the NMLU.

Following the Fitch affair a special delegate meeting of the union was held which decided to impose a levy on members in an attempt to meet outstanding claims, and to establish an age limit of 55 for new members qualifying for funeral benefit. (There was a report that the union's name was to be changed to the National Municipal and General Labourers' Union – possibly in order to broaden its base for recruitment – but this title was never used subsequently.)[18] The levy proved to be an unsuccessful method of raising the urgently needed money, despite appeals to members from Day, and resolutions from branches urging that the levy be 'strictly enforced'. In an attempt to save the situation another special meeting was held at which a further proposal for a levy was made, but this time it was rejected by the delegates. Meanwhile membership was falling; it numbered a little over 3,000 by the end of 1899, and with the branches in a state of demoralisation continuing losses were inevitable. In October 1899 the West Ham branch – a bastion of union strength – only narrowly voted against a proposal to secede to the Gas Workers' Union; Day and Will Steadman were at the meeting and may have influenced the vote. News that branch secretaries were simply refusing to be associated with the union any longer and were allowing their branches to collapse became commonplace. At Hackney, Camberwell and Westminster a more positive mood prevailed and each of these branches decided to break with the NMLU and register as independent unions, in this way they ensured that a decade of hard work did not go to waste.

With everybody abandoning the sinking ship, the inevitable happened in August 1900 when Day absconded with about £100 of the union's money. Like his predecessor he was none too successful, for he appeared in the City Courts in October where he pleaded guilty and offered no defence. He was ordered to pay the money back with a penalty of £2 or to serve three months in gaol.[19] A Hackney member, George Hibbard, was given the unenviable task of taking over as general secretary and one of the first actions of the executive following Hibbard's appointment was to cut his wages by three shillings a week. But by now it was too late for economies; branches were disbanding or seceding to other unions – principally the MEA – and the NMLU was rapidly nearing the end of its life. When the end eventually came, towards the end of 1900, the carcass of the NMLU was merely left where it stood, with outstanding debts in the region of £200. The Registrar of Friendly Societies was not informed of the collapse of the NMLU, probably because no official decision was ever taken by the members to wind it up – it was simply allowed to fade away.[20]

No public post-mortem ever took place over the body of the NMLU and its passing went unnoticed by London trade unionists. This was not because the NMLU had failed to register any successes during its existence, but rather that as the main role of organising municipal workers had already passed to the thriving MEA, a new era had opened and eyes were set on the future rather than on the past. But had trade unionists analysed the rise and fall of the NMLU they would have identified a number of crucial weaknesses which undermined the progress it had made.

First, and foremost, the NMLU crumbled because it was unable to cope with the financial problem of excessive funeral benefits from the time it first emerged in 1893. There were only two possible solutions to the problem: either increasing contributions, or reducing benefits – by cutting the level of benefit, applying an age limit or similar measure. Either of these approaches would have been unpopular with the members, many of whom had joined the union because they saw it as a cheap form of insurance. But, popular or not, action in this direction was the only way that the financial future of the union could have been guaranteed. Eventually decisions of the kind necessary were taken, but by then it was too late and the situation was irretrievable.

In its tactical approach, the NMLU's emphasis on winning elections to install sympathetic employers was both a strength and a weakness. It was successful in helping to establish Progressive and working class representation, but the central role it occupied in the union's activities developed at the expense of other forms of union activity. As a consequence, in local authorities where there was little or no chance of candidates sympathetic to the NMLU securing electoral dominance, the union had little to offer its members except protest meetings and similar activity aimed at winning public support. This may have had a marginal impact, but it made no real impression on the hard line Tory authorities and as a result the union was confronted with no-go areas – notably in the West End of London – throughout its existence.

The over-dependence by the NMLU on electoral activity was an extreme version of an attitude that emerged amongst many New Unionists – including Thorne and Burns – in the early 1890s, when they argued that at times strikes could be counter-productive, and that money used to finance strikes might be better used in securing labour representation. The exponents of this view were reacting to the obvious need for labour representation coupled with experiences of strikes which had ended in demoralisation and defeat and had provoked an employers' counter-offensive against union organisation. But Thorne and the other New Unionists never ruled out strike action in the way that the NMLU did; they recognised that the strike weapon was there for use if all else failed, whereas strike was not an option for the NMLU. Strike action against the reactionary local authorities could not have solved all of the NMLU's problems, but the NMLU never gave it serious consideration, let alone put it to the test.

Another weakness of the NMLU arose from its geographical concentration; throughout its life it remained London-based. It did have a sprinkling of branches in suburban areas but its core membership was employed in London vestries and – despite early aspirations to create a national union of municipal workers – there is no evidence that the NMLU made any attempt to realise those aspirations. The furthest it ever ventured outside London was to Caterham, in Surrey. To have developed beyond London would have been a big step for the NMLU, but the rewards could have been correspondingly great. Such a development was possible because small independent local unions had been established in various town and cities which could have been drawn together under the auspices of the NMLU. More important, there were thousands of municipal workers without union cards who could have been recruited by an organisation with the background and experience of the NMLU. The opportunity presented by this situation was not exploited until after 1904, and then by the MEA; but there was no reason why it could not have been achieved ten years before by the NMLU. A national organisation may have also acted against the blight of embezzlement which afflicted the union and which was certainly a major factor in its decline. Cole's dishonesty hit the union when it was on the rise and provoked a split in the ranks of municipal workers which was healed only when the NMLU collapsed and the workers regrouped in the MEA. Fitch and Day both took what they could out of the NMLU as it neared the end of its life, thereby hastening its inevitable demise.

In the light of the eventual collapse of the NMLU it would be easy to dwell only on its weaknesses, particularly the disastrous conduct of its general secretaries. But to do so would be to overlook the significant achievements made by the union in the course of its relatively short existence. The activities of the NMLU put municipal trade unionism on the map; it established the principle that unskilled manual workers employed by municipal authorities had a right to their own union and that combined in such a union they could produce results. The recruitment of 6,000 members by 1893 was a great achievement, and one which it took the MEA until 1904 to equal.

The NMLU won improvements in wages and conditions and by the turn of the century municipal workers could regard a living wage, sick-pay and annual holidays as rights to which they were entitled, not privileges dependent on the employers' generosity. Unskilled workers sought jobs with local authorities not only because such jobs guaranteed a degree of security but because they recognised that local authorities were becoming better employers. Work such as road sweeping had ceased to be the half-way stage to the workhouse and had become recognised as an essential occupation in the field of public health which needed to be undertaken by able-bodied men who had as much right as any other worker to a living wage. There is no doubt that the contribution by labour and Progressive politicians in raising what was described as the 'labour question' was crucial; but the intervention of the union on behalf of the workers themselves was the main dynamic force in winning improvements. On trades councils it was the municipal workers who most often advanced the demand that local authorities should be model employers and who helped to ensure that the labour question was on the agenda of local election committees and ranked high in the priorities of potential candidates. Where Progressive-controlled authorities failed to match their deeds with their promises it was activities by the NMLU and its allies which gave a sharp jolt to the memories of the people who had been elected on the promise of looking after the workers' interests. This role increased in importance as Progressive and labour representatives, naturally and correctly, concerned themselves with the broader issues of social reform – such as housing and education – and the danger arose that labour questions would be overlooked.

Less quantifiable than improvements in pay and conditions but just as important, was the contribution that the NMLU made to build the self-confidence and self-esteem of municipal employees, many of whom could not read or write.[21] The majority of workers enrolled by the NMLU performed jobs that were generally described as being 'the lowest of the low'; consequently the workers themselves were accorded a low status as individuals. Acceptance of this status by the workers led them to accept the idea that they did not deserve any better. By embracing the concept of trade unionism – with its principles of collective support – municipal workers equipped themselves with an ideology and practice that enabled them to transcend the old deferential attitudes that had been impressed on them and to assert themselves as valuable members of the community. The experiences of involvement in trade union organisational work, the ability to exert an influence on the behaviour of the employer and working alongside other trade unionists in local campaigns – all of these things helped to build the self-confidence of this generation of municipal workers. The schooling of the NMLU provided a formative and valuable experience which they took with them into future trade union activity – particularly in the MEA. Finally, by providing an effective alternative to the Gas Workers' Union, the NMLU established the principle that municipal workers were entitled to a union of their own rather than be engulfed by a general union. This principle was maintained strongly by the MEA, which was to have to live through major battles with the general unions in order to defend the idea of a single union for municipal workers.

NOTES

1. The survey recognises a discrepancy in totals between the number of unionists (4,500) and the total employed by municipal bodies (4,466). Previous estimates usually put the total nearer 10,000. C. Booth *Life and Labour of the People in London*, Second Series Vol 4, Industry London, 1903, pp. 44-5.
2. Ibid., Vol 5, Industry, p.15.
3. Ibid., Vol 4, Industry, pp. 44-45.
4. Booth MS Coll. Group A. Voll 26.
5. Booth, *Life and Labour* Vol 4, Industry, p.28. Fitch recognised that the wage raising policy of the NMLU had made it difficult for authorities to take on old men. Booth MS. Coll., Group B Vol 149.
6. This was recognised by the Progressive Newington Vestry in 1896/7 when they admitted that the improvements granted had occurred as a result of 'the force of public opinion brought about by the formation of the Newington Branch of the London (sic) Municipal Labour Union'. Annual Report of Newington Vestry 1896/7 p.49. See also the speech of John Burns at a meeting of the NMLU at Waterloo reported in *London*, 30 April 1896.
7. *London*, 4 March 1897. See also Beatrice Hewart 'The Wages of Vestry Employees', *The Economic Journal*, No. 31, September, 1898, Vol VIII.
8. *London*, 18 March 1897.
9. *London*, 12 August 1897.
10. *London*, 6 May 1897.
11. *London*, 14 January 1897.
12. LCC Annual Report, 1894.
13. *The Battersea Labour Gazette*, No. 3, 10 August 1890.
14. Where contractors were retained, problems would invariably arise as in Lambeth in 1906 where the firm removing dust were found to have underpaid their employees despite a council stipulation that five

shillings a day minimum be paid. The council were forced to replace the contractors and appeal to former employees of the firm to come forward and collect their share of the £1,000 unpaid wages. *Municipal Journal*, 13 July 1906. The area of local authority works departments (i.e. municipal intervention in the building industry) was, however, a more contentious issue around which major battles were to be fought. The LCC Works Department was a major issue in the elections of 1907 and 1910, it having been closed down by the Moderate majority in 1907.

15. See Fabian Tract No. 84 *The Economics of Direct Labour*, 1898, and J.W. Martin 'Direct Employment versus the Contract System' in *Municipal Affairs*, Vol II, No. 3, September 1898, New York, the latter being based heavily on the Fabian Tract written by Sidney Webb.

16. L. Fink, *Labour Politics and Political Culture; West Ham 1898-1900*, Harvard, 1970, (B.A. Dissertation) p.89.

17. Report of the case in *City Press*, 20 September 1899. It is not known whether Fitch went to prison or not. What scanty evidence exists appears contradictory. The sum of £300 would have been out of the reach of any working man to pay back in these years (assuming he had spent the money), and a scribbled note in the papers of the Registrar of Friendly Societies refers to an interview with Richards, one of the Union's Trustees which seems to indicate that a sentence was served. However, a reprinted letter in the NMLU EC minutes of 18 October 1899 from an insurance company acting on behalf of Fitch, refers to a sum of £20 being paid 'in settlement of this matter'.

18. *The Trade Unionist*, September 1899.

19. *City Press*, 3 October 1900.

20. See the correspondence in the Registrar of Friendly Societies File in the Public Records Office.

21. In 1891 the West Ham Borough Council had to abandon the practice of asking workers to sign for their wages because only 'a small percentage of men are able to sign their names' and so had to mark with a cross. West Ham Borough Council Minutes, 20 January 1891. This illiteracy could also be used for unscrupulous motives as in the case of St. Georges, Hanover Square Vestry in 1893, where following a memorial signed by two hundred and twenty workers asking for improvements, another memorial was drawn up and signed by one hundred and fifty-four men, saying that they were happy with their conditions. Seventy of the men who signed the second rogue petition later said they were unaware of its contents and wished to withdraw their support from it. Not surprisingly the Moderate-controlled Vestry decided to accept the second and ignore the first.
The Star, 7 December 1893.

7 The Formative Years

Although the passing of the NMLU attracted no public attention it is certain that one group of trade unionists followed events in the NMLU during its final phase of existence with more than a passing interest. Albin Taylor and his colleagues in the MEA must have been acutely aware that the imminent collapse of the NMLU presented a unique opportunity to recruit many new members – quickly and with little or no organisational expense. During the crisis months, individual members of the NMLU had been drifting over to the MEA, but the MEA wanted complete branch organisations of the NMLU to transfer their allegiance – and it did not have to wait long. When Herbert Day absconded with the funds a number of NMLU branches decided that enough was enough, and threw in their lot with the MEA. An appeal for loyalty to the NMLU from Day's successor, Hibbard, in October 1900, failed to stop the rot and by the end of the year virtually all NMLU branches had either collapsed, declared independence or seceded to the MEA. In all, approximately 500 NMLU members appear to have joined the MEA by the end of 1900.

Meanwhile, in March 1900, Taylor had pulled off something of a small coup when he persuaded the Battersea Vestry Workers to amalgamate with the MEA. At this time Battersea was very much the showpiece of the small independent municipal workers' unions; under the strong and able leadership of Albert Winfield it had well over 300 members who enjoyed the best wages and conditions in London. The strength of the Battersea Vestry Workers and Taylor's strong desire to incorporate them in the MEA were reflected in the terms of the amalgamation, which allowed Battersea to keep all of its existing funds in the new MEA branch and gave its members automatic entitlement to full MEA benefits. This was in contrast to following amalgamation agreements in which the smaller unions had to hand over a sum of money to guarantee MEA benefits to their members because in some cases there were discrepancies between MEA benefits and those of the smaller unions. These differences arose chiefly because in 1899, when the LCCEPA became the MEA, a graduated system of funeral benefits was introduced under which the £6 benefit – previously paid automatically – became payable only after six years' membership. The MEA had obviously learned the lesson of the financial consequences of the funeral benefits paid by the NMLU.

Taylor had apparently also done some re-thinking in other areas, because the rules of the MEA contained none of the class-based phrases which characterised the earlier rules of the LCCEPA; the MEA rules were written in sober, almost business-like tones which stressed the need to combine for mutual protection and advancement. It is difficult to judge whether this change of language reflected a wider and more important change in the union's strategy because no real evidence can be found – either before or after 1900 – of industrial militancy which could be used to measure attitudes. But what is certain is that the MEA, like the NMLU before it, did not regard strikes as an effective weapon; it considered the election of sympathetic representatives to local authorities as the most reliable method of improving members' pay and conditions.

It was not only the MEA that had recognised the value of political action to secure trade union objectives. Throughout the 1890s pressure had been growing inside the TUC for a trade union-led initiative to secure labour representation in parliament in order to give political expression to union activities. A stubborn rearguard action had been fought by the old guard of union leaders who still had faith in Liberal politics; but at the 1899 Congress the breakthrough came when a resolution was passed, by a very narrow majority, which called on the TUC to organise a conference of trade unions and socialist organisations to discuss ways of securing labour representation in parliament. The conference took place in London in February 1900 and was attended by 129 delegates; trade union delegates represented 500,000 members – less than half of the TUC's affiliated membership – and one of the smallest unions represented was the MEA, with Albin Taylor as its delegate. The conference decided to establish a Labour Representation Committee (LRC) which, in conjunction with local committees, would ensure that elections were fought with approved labour candidates. The MEA gave full support to this initiative by affiliating to the LRC nationally and encouraging its branches to become involved in local committees. The MEA also continued to pursue its activities in local authority elections by questioning candidates on aspects of union policy. At Hastings, for example, candidates were asked whether they supported minimum wage rates of 26 shillings for labourers and 30 shillings for parks staff together with annual holidays for all council employees; they were warned that the MEA had about 250 members in the town who would be urged to vote only for candidates who supported the union's demands.[1] Labour members of the LCC – such as Steadman, Crooks, Gosling, Dew and Cooper – who had previously been supported by the NMLU received continued union support from the MEA.

The impact that the MEA's local election strategy was making on London politics was demonstrated by influential articles published in *The Times* in 1902 which sharply attacked what was described as 'municipal socialism'. This meant the practice of Labour and Progressive councils pursuing policies of municipalisation, improved conditions for council employees and the use of direct labour in place of private contractors. *The Times* complained that these policies meant more jobs for municipal employees of a 'go easy character ... and in the matter of wages represents a privileged class'. The newspaper alleged that because local authority employees had a vested interest in re-electing members who would let them perform the minimum of work for inflated wages they would naturally do all in their power to support them at election times. Municipal employees, *The Times* continued, 'have discovered the use to which they can put their votes as a means of exploiting local government to their individual advantage'. Pointing with horror to the activities of the MEA in the electoral field, the article concluded that 'the only effectual way of checking the various evils ... would be to deprive corporation servants of their right to vote at municipal elections'.[2]

The articles in *The Times* were a public expression of the

continuation and intensification of the counter-offensive which the employers had launched against the unions in the 1890s. This reached a high point with the Taff Vale judgement of 1901, which held that unions were liable in law for financial damages suffered by employers during industrial disputes. It was a judgement which meant that while there was no law against strikes, any union which embarked on a strike placed its funds – and therefore its very existence – at risk. This judgement, more than any other factor, propelled unions into political activity and as a result the membership of the LRC nearly doubled during 1902. Even the most reticent unions recognised the threat posed to their survival by the Taff Vale judgement and accepted the need for political action through the LRC to establish – in parliament – union rights that had been undermined by the courts.

Despite the fact that it had been a prime target for attack by *The Times*, the MEA continued its vigorous intervention in local elections, each time posing to candidates the demand for a 30 shilling minimum wage in London and 28 shillings elsewhere, together with supplementary demands for annual holidays and sick-pay. At this time only Battersea could be said to measure up to the MEA's standards, and it was held up by the union as an example for others to follow. One authority which fell short of the MEA's requirements was the LCC which – despite its Progressive control and undeserved reputation – continued to be a thorn in the side of the union. Repeated attempts by Frank Smith and Will Steadman in 1901 to secure the 30 shilling minimum wage for all adult LCC employees were defeated, with leading Progressives arguing the case against pay increases.[3] John Benn said that if the LCC granted the minimum wage

> it would be impossible to place before the electors of London proposals to acquire any more of the tramway systems, and we may as well say goodbye to any further progress in the work of municipalising private undertakings.[4]

Sidney Webb, the leading light of Fabian socialism, also opposed the minimum wage and this provoked Taylor to write angrily in the Secretary's Report of 1902 that, 'the municipal employees of Deptford (Webb's seat) are asleep, and doing nothing to return a true friend of the poor'.

It is easy to appreciate Taylor's anger with the LCC and his frustration at being unable to shift its Progressive majority to meet the union's claims, because a high proportion of the MEA's membership was centred on the LCC, largely with main drainage and asylum employees but spreading to parks and gardens staff. The development of the tramways also provided a growth area for the MEA and it was quick to recruit drivers and conductors, an activity which spread beyond the LCC area to other towns. Throughout 1901 the MEA's membership grew rapidly and by the end of the year it reached more than 2,500 – an 80 per cent growth over the previous year – with branches established in Leicester, Derby and Bristol, and local unions at Hackney and Wimbledon joining the MEA ranks.

Although the union's membership was growing and its organisational base extending, Taylor still had what he described as 'great anxiety' about the union's financial viability and he warned members that funeral benefit was the largest single item of expenditure. Day-to-day expenses – including payments to Taylor – were low because Taylor was still employed full-time by the LCC at the Northern Outfall; but in the Annual Report of 1901 he said that the growth of the union created the need for a full-time officer to attend to its business efficiently – and he passed more than a hint that he was the man for the job. Stressing that members should be careful who they chose for a full-time post, he said the union needed someone, 'who has been tried and his past is well known – that is his public past'. The union did not want someone who was 'lazy dishonest or incompetent', what was needed was a 'practical man who will come from municipal service'. He warned that the employment of a full-time officer would be an expensive business because he would be expected to be, 'here, there and everywhere, mixing with all classes of society, councillors and officials ... so that the person whom you select should be well provided for'. Having set out this catalogue – coupled with more than a sprinkling of self advertisement – Taylor concluded by telling the members, 'much depends on your choice'.

Against the background of Taylor's proposal for the

appointment of a full-time officer – with its attendant cost – recruitment in the provinces became a priority for the union in 1902. Taylor and other officers, such as Albert Winfield, undertook week-long organising tours in the West Country, South Wales and the North West and branches were established in Cardiff, Swindon, Stockport and Manchester. But London still remained the centre of MEA activity, where the majority of members lived and worked, and for months on end contact with the growing number of provincial branches was maintained only by post. Under such conditions it was difficult for members outside London to share a common identity with an emergent national union, and the situation was made more difficult by a union rule which restricted membership of the Executive Council to those who lived within a 50 mile radius of London. This rule did not originate as an attempt to establish an exclusive role for London by barring outsiders from the union's principal body; it was merely a practical attempt to limit expenditure on travelling expenses which could have damaged the financial stability of the union in its early stages of development. However, the continued existence of the rule created difficulties for the union leaders who had to explain to members in the new branches outside London that while they had the right to vote in Executive elections they could only vote for someone who lived in London.

Another problem which rapidly surfaced as the MEA extended its activities beyond London was inter-union rivalry. In London there had been a strong base for unions recruiting exclusively amongst municipal workers for many years, and there was tacit acceptance of this form of organisation by the other unions. Outside London the situation, as the MEA discovered, was very different. In the provinces the general unions – particularly the Gas Workers' Union and the National Amalgamated Labour Union – regarded the organisation of municipal workers as their territory and when the MEA arrived on the scene conflict over recruitment rights was inevitable. An early example of this arose in Bristol when the affiliation of a recently established MEA branch to the local trades council was blocked by rival unions, out of what Taylor described as 'pure malice'.[5] In the 1901 Annual Report Taylor complained about the opposition to the MEA from

unions which were 'spreading slander' by 'trying to prejudice
the minds of representatives of the labour world'. He offered
£50 to anyone who could prove any of the allegations that had
been made against the MEA. Insisting that municipal
employees – like any other group of workers – had the right to
organise their union in any way they wished, Taylor argued
that the principle of organising on the basis of a common
employer was conducive to strong trade unionism. In an
attempt to establish this as a national principle, and thus
blunt the attacks of the general unions, the MEA submitted a
resolution on the subject to the 1902 annual Trades Union
Congress. Optimistically, the resolution sought the support of
delegates from other unions for a declaration that, 'no trade
union be represented which is not established by, and
confined its operations to a specific trade or industry'. Not
surprisingly – as it was a direct attack on the powerful general
unions – the resolution was not discussed by delegates; the
Standing Orders Committee ruled it out of order, presumably
to avoid a public row on the floor of Congress. However,
despite this tactic by the TUC, the conflict between the MEA
and the opposing unions was only just beginning – and in the
coming years it was to occupy the attention of the TUC on
many occasions.

In 1902, eleven of the MEA's 47 branches were outside
what is now known as the Greater London area.
Opportunities for membership growth still existed in London,
especially as the reputation of the union grew, but the real
potential for expansion was in the provincial towns and cities
where, despite activities by the general unions, thousands of
municipal workers had no contact with trade unionism. The
progress already made outside London, coupled with the
realisation of the potential membership that existed,
influenced the 1902 annual meeting of the MEA to follow
Taylor's advice to appoint a full-time officer. But, having
made a decision on the principle of the matter, delegates faced
the practical problem of defining the conditions on which the
appointment should be made and, with memories of the
earlier NMLU disasters clearly in their minds, the delegates
faced two issues. Firstly, there was the problem of recruiting a
full-time officer from a secure job elsewhere and placing him
in a post which – bearing in mind that the job was based on

the anticipation of expansion which had yet to be realised –
might prove to be only temporary. Secondly, there was a
strong fear of the possibility of the embezzlement of union
funds, a fear arising directly from the repeated experiences of
the NMLU. The influential Battersea branch attempted to
meet the practical problems involved. It proposed that the
appointment be on a three yearly basis – at a wage of 50
shillings a week until the membership rose to over 5,000 when
it would be increased to £3 a week. It added that,

> given the seriousness of taking someone from permanent
> employment which eventually may prove to be of a temporary
> character, the sum of £100 be put to one side for the purpose of
> giving such officer a start in life in the event of the society failing
> to meet its liabilities or being dissolved within three years.

The resolution continued with the caveat, 'such an
appointment and agreement being terminated should the EC
prove to an arbitration court, dishonourable conduct, or
insufficiency in the discharge of duties'.

The Battersea resolution seemed to solve all of the
problems, but Taylor – who was prime candidate for the post
and had been asked to leave the meeting while the matter was
discussed – declined to accept the job on the terms set out in
the resolution because its wording gave the Executive the
power to discharge the full-time officer with no right of appeal
to the rank and file members. Confronted with this situation
the delegates decided that they could not resolve the
differences and asked the Executive to seek a solution. A
further special conference was held in July 1902 when
proposals drawn up by the Executive were presented to
delegates. These proposals did not differ substantially from
the original Battersea resolution other than to stipulate that
the arbitrators should consist of an Executive appointee, an
officer appointee and the union's solicitor. Taylor was not, of
course, permitted to take part in the debate but many
delegates submitted amendments to the EC's proposals
designed to meet the points raised by Taylor at the previous
conference. These amendments accepted the proposal for the
£100 guarantee but said that the money should be lodged with
the arbitrators and paid to the full-time officer if the union

failed to meet its liabilities or should the officer be defeated in an election. The full-time officer would not be entitled to the guarantee if 'fraud or dishonesty, involving pecuniary loss to the society has been proved against him or gross neglect of duty'; the decision of the trustees was to be final in the event of any dispute. By an overwhelming vote of 64 to 9 the conference endorsed the amendments to the EC's report and Taylor was then appointed general secretary and organiser. This defeat by the conference delegates obviously upset the Executive because at its meeting in October it endeavoured to reverse the situation by deciding that in the future all decisions on the terms and conditions of full-time staff would be made by the EC alone. But this attempt to over-ride the rank and file was short-lived because six weeks later a subsequent delegate meeting rejected the Executive decision and reasserted the right of branch delegates to have a say in matters concerning the employment of full-time officers.

In his history of the General and Municipal Workers' Union, Hugh Clegg cites this long drawn-out process over the appointment of the MEA's general secretary as evidence that Taylor, 'seems to have anticipated trouble for a good deal of care was taken over the wording of his contract of employment'.[6] However, as has been recorded, the initial move in drawing up a tightly-worded contract did not come from Taylor. It came from the Battersea branch which – with the events of the NMLU fresh in its mind – feared two possibilities: that the union might be unable to meet its obligations to the general secretary or that the general secretary might fleece the union. Taylor responded to this initiative and tried to get the best terms and conditions he could. As he explained to the delegates, his objection to the original proposal was that it 'would place in the hands of a majority of the EC (or only five men) the power to discharge me, and take away the guarantee without my having the right of appealing even to the members of the society'. When the appointment was made in 1902 there was no question of any move against Taylor; he was regarded as the founder of the union and the rightful claimant to the job – as evidenced by the absence of opposing candidates. This was reinforced by the massive vote of support for the amended proposals at the July special conference which illustrated the support he enjoyed amongst the rank and file. What Taylor feared was not accountability and open trade union democracy, but the possibility of the formation of a hostile clique on the Executive which could use its position to dismiss him, leaving him little prospect of future work – especially when employers discovered that his previous job had been as a trade union official.

When Taylor was appointed as general secretary times were difficult for the trade union movement and as a result of the economic depression many unions were losing members. But the MEA fared comparatively well, with its membership growing from just over 3,000 in 1902 to well over double that figure by 1904. This growth not only reflected the stable nature of local authority employment but also the increase in the size of the municipal labour force, particularly in electricity and tramways which were expanding under municipal trading. The MEA set out to recruit amongst these new municipal employees and, considering the resistance it encountered, it enjoyed a remarkable degree of success. By the autumn of 1905 it could boast of 16 tramway branches; half of these were in the London area where the scope for recruitment increased as the LCC took over the lines from private companies. The take-over by the LCC was accompanied by a programme of electrification throughout the capital and this posed a threat of redundancy to many tramway workers, such as farriers and horse-keepers. Many workers lost their jobs, despite the efforts of the MEA and assurances from Progressive LCC members like John Benn that they would ensure that no redundancies took place; the LCC had again acted in a way which belied its reputation as a progressive local authority.

The MEA's success in recruiting tramway workers led to a conflict between it and the union which had previously enjoyed the leading role with that group of workers – the Amalgamated Association of Tramway and Vehicle Workers. During the inter-union wrangle that followed the Association sought to defend its territory by claiming that the MEA had no negotiating rights with the employers; but this argument did not convince the workers and they continued to join the MEA. The Association then changed its tactics and made an unsuccessful attempt to absorb the MEA with offers of amalgamation. The Gas Workers' Union also attempted to initiate discussion on the amalgamation of all labourers' unions during 1903; the MEA received an invitation but did not participate. The MEA's refusal to become involved in such an amalgamation was not surprising as it was forcibly asserting its right to organise municipal workers into a single union – the MEA – and meeting considerable hostility from the Gas Workers' Union as a consequence. The conflict between the two unions did not manifest itself only in local battles to recruit members; both unions also resorted to abuse and provocative taunting in their publications – with each condemning the other for trying to take the credit for pay increases won from the employers. The level to which the argument sometimes descended can be gauged from a sarcastic comment by Taylor when he wrote in the MEA monthly journal: 'the Secretary of the Gas Workers Union writes complaining of a municipal employee in Poplar leaving that Union to join this ... Ain't they getting angry?' The dispute reached almost farcical proportions at the 1903 annual TUC when Taylor opposed a resolution calling for a compulsory eight hour day on the grounds that he

> thought it undesirable that any one society should have charge of so important a subject. There was a danger that all those who objected to the principle of the resolution would be called traitors and all the rest of it.[7]

Taylor argued that a list should be published which showed all of those industries where the workers wanted the eight hour day because in some places it had already been achieved and bettered – and he cited the sewer flushers, who in some cases worked less than a 40 hour week. The arguments put forward by Taylor contained no good reasons for opposing a resolution calling for a general reduction in hours – especially as it had been the policy of the MEA for years. What prompted Taylor to oppose the resolution was not its content, but the fact that it was proposed by the Gas Workers' Union. Taylor's adversary in the TUC debate was Pete Curran, an organiser of the Gas Workers' Union, and the antagonism which the exchange generated was to have repercussions in a much more important TUC debate a few years later.

As part of its drive to recruit members in the unorganised sectors of municipal employment, the MEA turned its attention to the uniformed branches of the municipal services, where the workers were beginning to show sympathy towards trade unionism in response to a general undermining of their once supposedly superior status over manual workers. Firemen employed by the LCC were enrolled by the MEA early in 1905, and by the end of that year a separate branch was established for them. The LCC – with the Progressives still in control – reacted to this extension of trade unionism with hostility. Notices were posted in fire stations threatening to dismiss any fireman who failed to take any grievances he had directly to the Fire Officer in the first instance; the LCC was thus attempting to establish an alternative method to the MEA taking up problems on behalf of its members through trade union channels.[8] Will Steadman, a member of the LCC and MEA President since 1903, condemned this attempted victimisation in his annual address to union members in 1906, and proudly reported that not one fireman had left the MEA in the face of such threats. By this time the union had a substantial branch of between 400 and 500 firemen in London and had set up a new branch in Salford. But – despite its progress in recruiting new members and opening up new branches in many parts of the country – the union still had a fundamental weakness. This was clearly exposed when a dispute arose which involved another group of LCC uniformed employees – the park constables who patrolled the council's parks and open spaces. These workers were traditionally recruited from ex-policemen and ex-army NCOs; they defended their status jealousy and regarded themselves as superior to other workers in the parks, the symbol of this supposed superiority was the uniform issued by the council. When the LCC decided in July 1903 that – in order to save an estimated £1,650 a year in labour costs – all park constables should put on a working waistcoat and cap, roll up their sleeves, and collect litter every day there was an immediate uproar. Park constables were incensed at being asked to perform what they considered to be a menial task which had previously been undertaken by labourers, and very often casual labourers.

Some of the park constables were members of the MEA but

LCC park constables, Bostal Woods circa 1899

many were not, undoubtedly because they considered that their status placed them above membership of a trade union. However, faced with what they regarded as an unreasonable demand by the LCC they revolted and – almost to a man – refused to collect the litter; the council responded by suspending 51 of them. The union quickly convened a meeting of park constables and proposed that a deputation be elected to represent the various parks in London and, with Taylor as its spokesman, to put their case to the council's Parks Committee. The union then advised the men to resume work while awaiting the outcome of the deputation; it felt that such an action would help to convince the committee of the reasonableness of the men's case. With the exception of one man the park constables returned to work and reluctantly agreed to carry out the disputed litter collections while the deputation sorted out their problem, which they thought would take only a few weeks. Meanwhile expressions of support for the park constables flooded into the LCC from a broad cross-section of London's community. Resolutions passed at open-air park meetings organised by the Victoria Park Christian Evidence Association, the Protestant Forward Movement and the Protestant Laymen's Association were accompanied by letters from ratepayer's associations, trades councils and individuals. It was to be expected that trade unions and some individuals would object to the LCC's actions, but the surge of support from religious organisations was unusual and may well have reflected the religious habits of the park constables themselves.[9]

For its part the MEA appealed to its branches to subscribe to a fund which would be used to pay benefit to the park constables if they decided to come out on strike. But the brutal reality was that once the union had encouraged the men to return to work on the council's new terms the dispute was already lost. This was a fatal mistake by the MEA; while there may have been problems of morale amongst the men – as alluded to by Taylor – it was the union's duty, having intervened in the dispute, to build on the solidarity which had arisen when the men took spontaneous industrial action. The park constables were used to working in a disciplined situation, and with financial support and public backing they might well have effectively maintained their initial strike. But

LCC park keeper, Bostal Woods circa 1910

they were encouraged by the union to resume work under new conditions and to place all of their hopes on the success of the deputation to the LCC.

In the event the deputation was a complete and absolute failure. It did not meet the Parks Committee until three months after the dispute erupted. The committee referred the issue back to the General Sub-Committee which subsequently endorsed the council's previous decision and ordered the men to continue working under the new conditions. By any measure this was an abysmal failure for the MEA. In a belated effort to retrieve some of its lost credibility it made a claim for additional pay for the park constables on the grounds that they were now performing extra work. The claim received support from two labour members of the committee – Will Crooks and Ben Cooper, both supported financially by the MEA – but no progress was made and twelve months after it had started, the dispute was finally killed off in July 1904.

The experience of the park constables' dispute demon-strated that the strategy of the MEA suffered from the same fatal flaw as had the strategy of the NMLU in the 1890s. Once deputations, appeals to public opinion and 'striking through the ballot box' had failed to produce results, the union had no weapons left in its armoury since it was not prepared to promote, or even sanction, industrial action. Just how deep this attitude went in the MEA's philosophy was shown in 1905 when, in an appeal to workers to join its ranks, it said: 'We do not advocate strikes or lock-outs, but give our members their money back which would be used in this way in death benefits.' The weakness which this attitude engendered was again exposed when an anti-socialist alliance gained control of the West Ham Borough Council and rescinded the eight hour day which had been granted by the council in 1899. Big protest meetings were organised and strongly-worded resolutions were passed demanding the restoration of the eight hour day; predictably, these were simply ignored by the council. Will Thorne, of the Gas Workers' Union, took the opportunity to snipe – not without some justification – at the MEA, which had more members amongst West Ham Borough Council manual workers than any other union. Writing in the Gas Workers' Union report, Thorne accused the West Ham workers themselves of being somewhat responsible for this owing to their apathy and indifference to trade union principles. If all the men had been inside the pale of our organisation I do not think that we should allow the West Ham Council to take away the 8 hour day without a very fierce fight.[10]

Other unions also criticised the MEA and complained that they were being forced to compete against a union – and many MEA critics would not even have called it a union – which could afford to pay good cash benefits because it spent nothing in financing industrial action to win improvements in pay and conditions.

There was justification in these criticisms because by this time the emphasis in the MEA was not on building a fighting union – if it ever had been – but on consolidating existing conditions, making gains where possible by pressure and persuasion and supporting members with a wide range of friendly benefits. The importance of the latter activity was underlined by regular improvements in the death benefit and the introduction of accident benefits and a legal aid scheme. There was further criticism of the MEA for its alleged insularity and self-interest at the expense of wider trade union solidarity over a campaign it launched, in 1902, to standardise pension entitlements of local authority employees. Things came to a head after the union had drawn up a draft Parliamentary Bill and circulated it to MPs and local authorities in an effort to win their support. Delegates to the 1904 annual TUC discussed the MEA's approach and, by an overwhelming majority, rejected it on the grounds that the TUC was seeking a comprehensive pension scheme for all workers who reached the age of 60, and the MEA's go-it-alone campaign for a separate arrangements for local authority workers would weaken the general campaign for old age pensions.[11]

However, despite the general weakness of the MEA's over-reliance on political action to secure improvements in pay and conditions, the strategy did have some limited success. By early 1904 the union had established its minimum pay rate of 30 shillings in five London borough councils (which had taken over local authority administration from the vestries in 1900) and two urban district councils outside London. It was no coincidence that all of these councils had returned Progressive majorities in local elections during which the MEA had waged a big campaign to secure the election of sympathetic representatives. In addition to allocating more than £40 to branches to assist with local election expenses and issuing standard questions to be put to candidates in order to test their attitudes to labour questions, the MEA also got the London Trades Council to call on all labour candidates to pledge their support for wages and conditions equal to any other – which meant the best – metropolitan borough council. Clearly, the MEA was determined to play its part in building labour representation – particularly in the London area – as a way of improving its members' conditions. However, even with the emphasis that the MEA leadership placed on the importance of labour representation, difficulties arose in persuading members to pay their contributions to the special political levy. So bad did the situation become that in March 1904 the MEA had to withdraw temporarily from the Labour Representation Committee because of inadequate funds. To their credit a number of branches – including those newly formed in Scotland – insisted on maintaining their payments through local committees, and in this way the MEA's links with the LRC were maintained.

Financial considerations undoubtedly weighed heavily on the minds of the MEA Executive during 1904 because although membership had grown rapidly so had expenses, particularly victimisation benefit according to delegates to the Annual Meeting who claimed that it was one of the major problems facing the union. It is clear that a number of branch secretaries were dismissed by their employers, and the union – undoubtedly because it would not take strike action even to defend its activists – felt powerless to do anything other than pay benefit and to make the plaintive plea to members in its *Quarterly* report: 'Can any friend find them employment?' The dismissal of branch secretaries was not the only financial problem facing members; diminishing and disappearing branch funds – the old problem of embezzlement repeated itself, but this time at local level. As early as 1901 Taylor had found it necessary to tell branch secretaries that the Executive would 'put down pilfering with a strong hand', and to warn that offenders could, 'expect no mercy from us'. Nevertheless, during the next few years Taylor was forced to travel to many parts of the country, to 'put branches right', after local union funds had disappeared. In most cases the money was retrieved without the members responsible facing the 'ignominy of imprisonment', but in a few cases the offenders were taken to court and forced to either repay the money or face imprisonment. Branch members were encouraged by the Executive to be vigilant with their branch officers in money matters and to insist on regular financial reports. This approach, Executive chairman Albert Winfield said, would help to avoid the 'taint which, of all, is the most damaging to the reputation of a trade union'.

But, whatever its short-term financial problems, the union continued to expand in size and influence as the decision to appoint Taylor as full-time general secretary paid dividends. The objective of recruiting unorganised municipal workers throughout the country was being realised and branches were established as far apart as Portsmouth and York. Taylor was sent on organising tours around the country and the Executive expected positive results – in the shape of new branches – on his return. But this growth contained a built-in contradiction as it meant more and more work for the general secretary which he found increasingly difficult to cope with, and he tried on more than one occasion – without success – to secure the appointment of an assistant. In July 1904, after a branch ballot of members, it was eventually agreed to appoint a full-time organiser and the Executive Council considered eight candidates for the post. After each of the candidates had addressed the Executive for twenty minutes – without notes – the EC selected two, Albert Winfield and Richard Davies from Leicester, as being equally suitable for appointment and said that it was impossible to choose between them. The deadlock was resolved when Winfield stood down and allowed Davies to be appointed.

Reliable facts on Davies's background are hard to establish. At the time of his appointment as full-time organiser he was said to be the chairman of the Leicester Branch of the MEA, but he was not a municipal worker. In a declaration before being elected to the Leicester City Corporation in 1904 he gave his occupation as a newspaper editor, but there is no trace of the newspaper for which he worked. Taylor later said that before his appointment as MEA organiser, Davies had worked for the Shop Assistants' Union in South Wales and the Navvies' Union and according to Taylor, both of these unions had dismissed him. But these subsequent accusations were made by Taylor in a very heavily-charged situation when the two men were in conflict. What is clear, as Taylor himself admitted, is that Davies was an accomplished individual who so impressed Taylor on their first meeting that Taylor asked him to consider becoming an MEA organiser.

The effectiveness of Davies as an organiser was demonstrated in the first few months of his work with the MEA, which he spent in Glasgow recruiting members and setting up new branches. By the end of September 1904, nine branches with 1,500 members had been established in the city – a remarkable achievement by any standards of the MEA. Among the new recruits were roadsweepers, former members of the Scottish Carters' Union who joined the MEA on agreed terms, and approximately 100 members of the Glasgow Main Pipe Layers' and Jointers' Association, which had also amalgamated with the MEA. So impressive were the results of Davies's activities in Scotland that at the end of 1904 the union's Executive decided that the MEA was sufficiently well established there to merit the appointment of a full-time district secretary, and John Martin, who had been secretary of the Pipe Layers' Association, was made the first full-time regional officer of the MEA on a wage of 45 shillings a week.

Following this breakthrough in Scotland, other developments followed rapidly. In January 1905 the Hull Corporation Employees' Protection Society agreed to amalgamate with the MEA; it was linked with new branches that had been established in Yorkshire and North Lincolnshire to form a Northern and Midland District and the Executive appointed another full-time district secretary to handle union affairs there. Peter Tevenan, formerly secretary of the Stockport branch, was appointed to the post, having resigned from his job as Borough Auditor which he had taken up only a few months earlier. As with Davies, little is known about Tevenan's background. It is known that he had worked for the Amalgamated Society of Railway Servants in Ireland during the late 1890s and Taylor subsequently alleged that Tevenan had been dismissed from this post 'for a very grave offence'.[12] That Taylor could make such an allegation raised speculation about the criteria adopted, and methods used, by the MEA Executive when it was appointing officers. In the following months two more districts were established by the EC: the South Western and Wales District with Richard Davies acting as secretary and the London District, with Albert Winfield as secretary.

At this stage the MEA was clearly outgrowing its old geographical base in London and was rapidly developing an informal national structure. The need arose to integrate this informal administrative arrangement into the formal constitutional organisation of the union and at the 1905 Annual Meeting the structure of the union was officially divided into Districts, with semi-autonomous District Conferences given the power to elect representatives to the Executive Council. This new arrangement not only reduced the size of the Executive but also made a very important change in its character and composition. The London monopoly of Executive power, which had existed since the union was first set up, came to an end and the MEA took on a national organisational form which matched the dimension of its membership.

Soon after this organisational change the MEA made its last substantial amalgamation with another union when, in November 1905, the Belfast Municipal Employees and Other Workers' Society with 600 members joined the MEA. Andrew Boyd, the former secretary of the Society, became secretary of the new MEA District and under his leadership the union grew rapidly and by the autumn of 1906 there were four branches in the city. Although the scope for any significant amalgamations narrowed after the Belfast Society linked up with the MEA, Taylor and his colleagues continued to advocate the principle of one union for all municipal employees and in pursuing this principle they encouraged the remaining smaller societies to join the MEA. In June 1906 the Camberwell Municipal Labour Union, after six years of independence, joined the MEA. This amalgamation – though not significant in terms of numbers of members – symbolised the changing fortunes of municipal workers' trade unions. The MEA had grown, very slowly at first, from a breakaway of the NMLU into a national organisation with more than 15,000 members; with the amalgamation of the Camberwell Municipal Labour Union the MEA was joined by a group of workers which contained some of the pioneers of municipal workers' trade unionism back in October 1889. It was an important landmark in the development of the MEA, establishing not only its leading role as the union for municipal workers but also strengthening its historical continuity with the pioneers. Fulfilling this role the MEA continued to expand and its membership rose to 16,000 in 1906. New branches were established in small provincial towns, but by far the most effective development was in the large industrial conurbations. By September 1906 there were nineteen branches in Manchester, eight in Salford, eighteen in Glasgow, four in Belfast, four in Edinburgh and four in Newcastle. But – although the balance was shifting – the largest concentration of membership remained in London, which had 77 branches out of a national total of 158.

The strength of the MEA's membership in London was matched by the strong position of London municipal workers in the national wages league, where they remained at the top of the table. A government survey of 1906 revealed that London municipal workers were, on average, at least four shillings a week better off than their best paid counterparts in the provinces. The survey also showed that the size of a local authority influenced the level of wages. For example, in towns with a population of more than 100,000 only one in a hundred roadsweepers earned less than £1 a week, while in the smaller towns more than a quarter were below this level. In the worst position were some 200,000 workers – mostly roadworkers – employed by county and rural district councils, with more than 60 per cent receiving wages of less than £1 a week. Wages in these country areas were largely determined by the level of pay of agricultural labourers, which was notoriously bad.[13] The MEA, in common with all unions, failed to appreciate this problem and neglected the county roadmen – a neglect which persisted for another thirty years.

Prompted largely by the success of the MEA, the hostility between the MEA and rival unions intensified, especially as the Gas Workers' Union became aware that the momentum which the MEA was building could threaten the existence of its own municipal branches.[14] The situation came to a head at the 1906 Trades Union Congress in Liverpool when the National Amalgamated Labour Union together with the Gas Workers' Union put before delegates a resolution which condemned those organisational forms of trade unionism, which, it alleged, sought to divide workers in the public sector from those in the private sector, and called on the TUC to 'use its best endeavours to prevent the spread of such methods of organisation'. This was clearly an attack on the MEA and its advocacy of a single union for municipal workers. During an acrimonious debate allegations were made that the MEA was poaching members from the NALU, the Printers Warehousemen, and the Tramway and Vehicle Workers. Pete Curran, of the Gas Workers, caused an uproar when he claimed that 'agents of the association' were visiting towns and intimidating labour councillors to induce council employees to leave other unions and join the MEA. When challenged to produce evidence, Curran said that he had spoken to an alderman from Huddersfield who had told him of this practice. At this point the MEA delegation should have been able to call on Taylor to act as their champion, and also to personally defend himself as he was the 'agent' referred to by Curran; but Taylor was not present – he had been taken ill and had left the Congress.

In the absence of Taylor it was left to Albert Winfield to move an MEA amendment to the resolution and Jones, Manchester district secretary of the MEA, to second it. Their task was not easy because the amendment was very provocatively worded; it sought to change the resolution by deleting the statement that the organisation of municipal workers in one union was detrimental to the 'best interests of Trade Unionism', and substituting that it was detrimental to the 'financial interests' of NALU, the Gas Workers' Union, and the Tramway Workers' Union. The implication was that the sectional interests of these three unions could not be equated with the interests of trade unionism as a whole. Despite this attempt at cleverly-applied tactics by the MEA it became clear during the debate that the union was not going to make much headway, especially when allegations were made that the MEA had tried to recruit mechanics – thus infringing the rights of the prestigious Amalgamated Society of Engineers. In the MEA's defence, Winfield and Jones quoted its record and asked why municipal workers could not have their own union – as did the miners and the postal workers. Supporting his colleagues, Peter Tevenan struck at the central issue when he said that the union had existed since 1894 and not a word had been said against it until it became successful in recruiting previously unorganised workers; general unions were now attacking the MEA and, 'we are told we have no right to live'. One of the most telling speeches came from a delegate from the Army Clothing Union who, in defence of his own union and the MEA, said:

> Until you have a national organisation of unskilled labour, you have no right to object to anyone doing the work of organisation. You have no right to protest us organising a body of men who have never been organised before ... might I suggest to the Gas Workers that they should turn out those members in their union who are clerks and carmen. Let them join the Union of Clerks and the Carmen's Union.[15]

But whatever points were scored during the debate the big battalions ranged against the MEA were too strong in numbers for the union to make any impression. When the votes were called the MEA amendment was rejected by 1,196,000 votes to 42,000 and the original resolution was passed overwhelmingly. Following this decision at Congress the TUC circulated all unions and trades councils with a devastating statement which said that municipal employees' societies, 'would have a weakening and disintegrating effect upon the forces of organised labour ... [and] would destroy the benefits of united trade unionism'.[16] This TUC directive made it extremely difficult – as it was intended – for the MEA to function in areas where it experienced opposition or hostility from other unions. Opponents of the MEA could now claim the support of official TUC policy. Through the TUC the general unions had struck a damaging blow at the MEA, but the harm that had been done was insignificant compared to the savage injuries that the MEA was about to inflict upon itself.

NOTES

1. Letter from Taylor to Hastings Borough Council Candidates, 1902, (GMBATU Archive).
2. *The Times*, 10 September 1902. For a reply to the articles and an exposure of the links between the author and the free enterprise lobbying group – the Industrial Freedom League – see *Municipal Journal*, 17 October 1902.
3. Minutes of LCC 14 May; 8 October; 15 October 1901.
4. Quoted in A.G. Gardiner, *John Benn and the Progressive Movement*, London, 1925, p.240.
5. Letter from A. Taylor to Bristol Trades Council Secretary, 1901, (GMBATU Archive).
6. H. Clegg, *A General Union in a Changing Society*, Oxford, 1964, p.60.
7. Annual Report of TUC, 1903.
8. LCC Fire Brigade Committee Minutes, 5 October 1905; 5 April 1906.
9. See LCC Parks Committee Minutes and Presented Papers for meetings of October to December.
10. Quarterly Report and Balance Sheet of the NUG & GL, June – September, 1903.
11. Annual Report of TUC, 1904.
12. Tevenan was ASRS secretary for Ireland in 1897/8 and was dismissed because of misconduct. Report of AGM of ASRS, 4-7 October 1898. We are grateful to Dr P. Bagwell for this reference.
13. 'Report of an Enquiry by the Board of Trade into the earnings and hours of work of workpeople in the UK. Part IV Public Utility Services' Parliamentary Papers, 1910 (84).
14. In 1906 there were ten municipal branches of the Gas Workers' Union and there would have been many other municipal workers in general branches. Quarterly Report and Balance Sheet of NUG & GL December, 1905 – March, 1906.
15. Annual Report of TUC, 1906.
16. Annual Report of TUC, 1908.

8 Dissent and Division

While the MEA was having its public battle with rival unions it was also locked into a private internal battle. There is no evidence to suggest that the two were directly related, but it is unlikely that the MEA's rivals – the general unions – were completely unaware of the division that were opening up in the MEA's leadership. It is quite possible that knowledge of the MEA's internal problems may have influenced the timing of the general unions' attack on the MEA at the 1906 TUC. The historical fact remains that the coincidence of these two events generated a damaging force which had a devastating impact on the MEA.

As is frequently the case in such situations, most of the surviving historical evidence of the rift in the MEA's leadership presents the partisan views of those intimately involved in the dispute – and much of it was produced subsequent to the actual events in order to influence the attitudes of rank and file members.[1] But, so far as can be ascertained, it appears that the internal problems of the MEA began as a relatively minor issue late in 1905 when Taylor received a complaint from one of the Manchester branches about the conduct of its then full-time district secretary, Peter Tevenan. The branch alleged that Tevenan had borrowed money from a member and had not returned it; the branch also alleged that Tevenan had improperly processed a grievance by paying a member three days' wages without consulting the union's head office. When Taylor wrote to Tevenan on these matters he added a complaint of his own; Tevenan's expenses were apparently excessive and required an explanation. Taylor concluded with the comment: 'On the face of this the whole thing appears to be very irregular.'

There is no record of Tevenan's response, but it cannot have been particularly convincing because in February 1906 the Executive passed a vote of censure on Tevenan for, 'neglect of duty, borrowing money from the Secretary of the Manchester No 2 Branch and ordering money to be paid other than by rule'. From this point on the situation deteriorated. Taylor wrote to Tevenan asking for an explanation as to why he (Taylor) had known nothing of a series of meetings organised by Tevenan until an invoice for the printing of leaflets had arrived at head office. Letters of complaint against Tevenan also came from branches and included various allegations: that he had not accounted properly for money given to him by branch secretaries; that he had claimed a positive response from an interview with a Manchester fire officer when no such interview had taken place – a case of the union 'fouling our own nest and turning friends into enemies', commented the branch secretary; and that Tevenan had attended a meeting in an intoxicated condition. These allegations were considered by the Executive in October 1906 and the minutes of the meeting record that Tevenan accepted some of the complaints against him but rejected others. The Executive decided to pursue the matter by asking for an auditor's report on Tevenan's expenses and instructing Taylor to make further investigations into the allegations.

When the auditor's report was produced it concluded:

> the North Eastern District Secretary's organising expenses are excessive because they are nearly double his wages, he having booked 80 days lodgings at 7/6 a day, there being only 91 days in the quarter including Sundays.

Alongside Taylor's report on the other complaints this was evidence enough for the Executive and at its meeting in December 1906 it decided to dismiss Tevenan. It was a decision which sparked off an extraordinary chain of events.

On learning of the Executive's decision to dismiss him, Tevenan apparently established some form of breakaway organisation under the name of the Corporation Workmen's Union of Great Britain from his base in the North East. Taylor was sufficiently worried about the prospect of MEA members seceding to this organisation in the North East to send Albert Winfield to Hull, Grimsby and Scarborough to fly the flag and consolidate the MEA's position. Richard Davies, who at this time was based in Scotland, was moved down to Newcastle by

Taylor on the same mission. According to Taylor, however, Davies did not go to Newcastle; instead he went to Middlesbrough in order to meet Tevenan and then – again according to Taylor – went to Leicester to talk to the chairman of the MEA Executive, Richard Baldwin. At this meeting Davies suggested that Tevenan should be re-instated, that the MEA should pay the expenses of floating the breakaway union and that Taylor should be asked to resign for his role in the affair. The arguments presented to the chairman of the Executive by Davies must have been persuasive, because at its next meeting, in January 1907, the Executive made a dramatic change in its position. It decided to reinstate Tevenan, to make a grant of £50 towards the expenses incurred in establishing the breakaway union and to refer the whole matter to the MEA's annual conference for ratification.

The dispute then gathered a momentum of its own, with branches submitting resolutions calling for Taylor's resignation which, according to Taylor's account, were the result of continuing hostility whipped up by Davies. The Executive took the matter very seriously and held a special meeting in February 1907 to consider 'the actions of the general secretary'. Three complaints were laid against Taylor at this meeting: firstly, that he acted in defiance of the Executive Council; secondly, that he had issued malicious circulars which vilified members of the Executive and the union's officers and generally misrepresented the union, and thirdly, that he had failed to advise the Executive of the methods to be adopted in connection with the rules of the union. In addition, two resolutions were submitted for the meeting. The first, from the Irish District, called on the Executive to take whatever action it felt was necessary to deal with Taylor following his behaviour in relation to the North Eastern District. The second, from the London District, urged the Executive to stand by Taylor until serious charges had been proved against him. Taylor was given the opportunity to put his arguments to the EC, but no record exists of what was said at the meeting. Whatever Taylor said proved to be of no avail. The Executive approved by a two to one majority, a resolution put by Scottish EC member Turner and seconded by South West EC Member Spencer, to suspend Taylor from office as general secretary. As if to underline the significance of its decision, the EC then appointed Taylor's arch rival Davies to act as temporary general secretary. Having taken this serious step the Executive sought to consolidate its position among the members by convening a special conference in Manchester on 15 March, to be attended by four delegates from each district.

Although he was the central figure in this unfolding drama, Taylor claimed that he did not receive any written notice of the charges against him until the morning of the conference itself. He was then presented with a list of 22 charges which he claimed had been drawn up by Davies in advance and presented to the Executive on the same morning for rubber stamping. Taylor also argued that the conference was unbalanced in its composition because the London District, with 7,000 members, had only four delegates while the remaining five districts, with a total of 7,000 members amongst them, were represented by a total of 20 delegates.

After a session lasting 13 hours the conference delegates voted to endorse the Executive's decision to suspend Taylor. But the margin of support for the EC was narrow – with eleven delegates backing the Executive, ten voting against and three abstaining. A breakdown of votes shows that Taylor collected four from London, four from Manchester and two from the South West – the other two delegates from this district being amongst the abstainers. This distribution of votes reflects Taylor's areas of support in the country; London was his historical base, where he had made his name as a trade union pioneer; Manchester was where Tevenan had been an unpopular district secretary; and the South West of England was well known to Taylor, where he was acting district secretary. Taylor later complained that the vote which had produced the knife-edge result had been taken in an atmosphere of confusion but, despite 'stout protests', the decision had been declared final. The minutes of the meeting record only the decisions taken, but Taylor claimed that there had been little chance of real discussion by delegates on the floor of the conference because most of the time had been taken up by Davies making his charges and Taylor responding to them.

Following the Manchester conference Taylor and his

MUNICIPAL WORKERS' SOCIETY

Offices—7, Thorpe Road, East Ham, E.

Re SUSPENSION OF Mr. A. TAYLOR.

We, the Executive Council of the above Society, having considered the Report issued by the M.E.A. on the above matter, have decided to treat the same with the contempt it deserves, except to say we have determined to stand by Mr. Taylor until it is proved to an impartial tribunal that he has committed fraud, grossly neglected his duties, or other serious charges.

They boast that the action of the N.E.C. was confirmed at Manchester by a majority. They do not state the figures, which are 11 for and 10 against. The 10 were London, Western and Manchester Districts, where there were about 11,000 members.

We have determined to establish the above Society for the following among other reasons :—

1. The unfair and unjust way Mr. Taylor, the Founder of the M.E.A., has been treated by the N.E.C. of that body, without written and signed charges.

2. To prevent a recurrence of this kind of thing, with the enormous expense and grave unrest amongst the members.

3. To make a more democratic Society, with a much larger E.C., so as to have control by the members.

A friend of the M.E.A. wrote to each member of the N.E.C. suggesting that this dispute should be referred to arbitration   This friendly suggestion was met by expelling their founder, stopping his wages, ordering him out of house, refused to give up a cupboard, press, and other office requisites made by Mr. Taylor years ago to save the members' money. **How brutal and unkind.** Compare this with their action in the North Eastern District.

The Gen. Secretary (pro. tem.) has issued a threatening letter to the Branches (more than one) of the Municipal Workers' Society in which he states : " The National Executive Council of the M.E.A. will not try to hinder any Branch from seceding and following Mr. Taylor."

We ask all Members to come and join the Municipal Workers' Society, thereby support the leader you know so well.

All Benefits are guaranteed as though nothing had happened.

" Ring out the old, ring in the new, Reject the false, support the true."

We are, fellow Municipal Servants,

J. J. BRADLEY.	A. W. HALL.
C. G. ROSE.	H. COULLING.
J. TONKS.	J. RADBURN.
G. E. POLLEY.	W. CONQUER.
N. G. GREEN.	J. F. HART, *Chairman.*
	A. TAYLOR, *General Secretary.*

One of the many handbills issued by Taylor
during the dispute with the MEA, 1907

supporters in the MEA immediately planned a counter-offensive which was launched ten days later at a conference attended by 35 London branches representing a total of 4,500 MEA members. This conference set in motion the final and irreversible act in Taylor's relations with his old union when it decided to secede from the MEA and to establish a new organisation to be known as the Municipal Workers' Society. The Executive of the MEA was quick to respond to this challenge. Five days after the meeting of Taylor's supporters it expelled him from the MEA, decided to take legal proceedings to retrieve money and property from any branch secretary whose branch defected to the new union, and sanctioned the expenditure of £100 to combat Taylor and prevent the secession of MEA branches. For his part, Taylor issued leaflets – as general secretary of the Municipal Workers' Society – putting his side of the argument and appealing to members of the MEA to join the MWS. He also gave the guarantee that the new union would meet all benefit commitments accrued in the MEA – a bold move for an infant organisation with no financial resources. Predictably, a large number of London MEA branches immediately moved over to the Municipal Workers' Society, as did five West Country branches. But the MEA managed to retain the bulk of its members – approximately 11,500 against the 3,500 who had decided to join Taylor.

The MEA made considerable efforts to undermine Taylor's activities and to stem the growth of the newly-formed union. It even managed to force a change of name on the new organisation by protesting to the Registrar of Friendly Societies that the title Municipal Workers' Society was too much like the Municipal Employees' Association; the Registrar upheld the protest and this caused Taylor and his colleagues to adopt the title of the National Union of Corporation Workers. Davies was also instructed by the Executive of the MEA to contest the claim by Taylor for the £100 guarantee made to him by the union in 1902. It took several months before the matter was finally resolved by three arbitrators – Will Steadman, the MEA solicitor and Fred Hoare, a union trustee – as provided for in the agreement. At the arbitration Davies argued that Taylor had not been dismissed but had expelled himself by establishing a rival union and was therefore not entitled to the £100 under the terms of the guarantee. In his defence, Taylor established that before he had set up the new union he had been refused wages by the MEA and had been told by Davies to leave the MEA offices because there was no place for him; it was also established that Taylor had not been guilty of gross neglect of duty. Consequently the arbitrators decided that the MEA should pay the £100 guarantee plus legal costs to Taylor. Legally Taylor had been vindicated and he claimed victory. But the MEA, in its 1909 Annual Report, also claimed victory when it recorded that Taylor was to cease his campaign against the MEA. In reality, the victors were those who wanted to halt the growth of trade union membership amongst municipal workers.

Both during and after the dispute Taylor issued a mass of literature in which he consistently claimed that the charges made against him had never been proved. Indeed, he argued that the charges had, in fact, only been formulated after he had been suspended from his post as MEA general secretary. In making this allegation Taylor was probably referring to a detailed eight-page statement issued by the MEA Executive after the Manchester conference had endorsed the decision to suspend him. The statement summarised events from the standpoint of the Executive and in seeking to win mass membership support for the NEC and conference decision it inevitably exploited every possible complaint against Taylor. It did, however, set out in some detail the major points of conflict between Taylor and the Executive and showed how a situation had arisen which made it impossible for the union to continue to function effectively.

The low level to which relationships between Taylor and the NEC had sunk was demonstrated in the Executive statement when it reproduced a letter sent by Taylor, as MEA general secretary, to the union's full-time district secretaries in February 1906. Taylor's letter was written after the NEC had decided to keep a tighter check on the expenses and activities of full-time officials, a decision doubtless prompted by the complaints about Tevenan which had just been discussed by the Executive. In his letter Taylor, obviously in an extremely angry mood, said the Executive had taken this decision in spite of his opposition and as a result, 'they are well on the way to smashing up the Society, through internal snarling.' For a general secretary to make such an attack on his elected Executive in a letter to full-time officials was – to say the very least – a reckless action incompatible with the standards of behaviour the Executive was entitled to expect from the senior full-time official of the union. But Taylor's recklessness did not stop at this point; his letter continued to say that there was only one way to deal with the Executive members, 'that is to try and get other men elected in their places at the approaching election and I think it would be well to change them once a year'. This was an astonishing suggestion for a general secretary to make to full-time officers, even if it was only as an angry reaction. But Taylor compounded it by telling the full-time officers how to go about the practical business of replacing existing Executive members.

> If you agree with me, will you kindly look out for a decent man, get him nominated, and pull the wires to secure his election. Let me know who you fix upon so that I can help if the opportunity offers.

As if compelled by a desire for self-destruction, Taylor concluded his letter by telling the district secretaries that the Executive members, 'give me the Damn sick'.

The letter was an absolute gift to Taylor's opponents and, inevitably, it was produced at the Manchester conference as a prime piece of evidence against him. The Executive, in its statement to members after the conference, drew attention to the fact that no copy of the letter existed at head office and added the thrust, 'but a leaf is missing from the letter book about that date'. Taylor did not deny writing the letter; he admitted to making a mistake, he said, and had withdrawn it. But this admission failed to impress the Executive which used the letter as an example of how Taylor had attempted to 'destroy the authority of the NEC'.

The Executive statement to members also made a clear link between the internal dispute in the MEA and the 1906 TUC resolution aimed at the union. It said that Taylor's actions in connection with the resolution had 'displayed lack of ability and caused great injury to the Society'. The statement said that Taylor had submitted an amendment to the TUC –

without the approval of the MEA Executive – which sneered at 'other well known and old established trade unions', and would 'estrange support from our Society'. The Executive said that Taylor had issued a circular to every TUC delegate in which he attacked the unions mentioned in the amendment, that he had refused to withdraw 'his obnoxious amendment' despite the advice of the other three MEA delegates to the TUC (three full-time district secretaries), and that – on the grounds of ill-health – he had left the Congress on the day that the resolution and amendment were being debated, taking with him all the relevant documents and leaving the MEA delgates without instructions. 'In consequence of this action they were unable to meet the attacks of their opponents,' said the Executive. In considering these charges against Taylor it must be remembered that the MEA Executive made its comments in hindsight – months after the TUC resolution had been passed – and it may well have began seeking to deflect the responsibility for the affair away from the MEA and on to Taylor, in the hopes of reaching an accommodation with the TUC and the general unions.

Amongst the other charges levelled against Taylor in the Executive statement there were two general complaints which helped to put the whole dispute into perspective. The first was that Taylor was guilty of 'neglecting and disobeying the orders of the National Executive Council'. The second was that Taylor's conduct of affairs at the union's head office and general administration, 'prove him incapable of discharging the duties of the Chief Executive Officer of a large and growing Society'. Both of these charges were illustrated in the Executive statement with examples of actions by Taylor – some of which appear serious while others seem to border on the trivial – which the EC considered gave support to its case for Taylor's suspension.

Any assessment of the rights and wrongs in the dispute between Taylor and the MEA Executive must be set in an historical context which takes fully into account the objective factors which existed at that time and which determined the environment in which both Taylor and the Executive operated. The most important of these was the very rapid growth in the size and geographical spread of the union in a short period of time; since the turn of the century the MEA had grown from a small London-based union into a large – and still expanding – organisation with branches developing in all parts of the country. This growth had, in turn, changed the internal character of the union. In place of a localised organisation with Taylor as its focal point it had developed a national character, with a representative Executive Council and full-time district secretaries evolving as power bases away from the union's centre in London. In external relations, too, the rapid expansion of the MEA had created a new situation as its aggressive recruiting activities made an impact on the areas which other well-established unions considered to be their natural territory. All of these factors were affecting the MEA within a wider social, political and economic environment in which the labour movement – in parliament and in the country at large – was playing an ever-growing role in public affairs. The combination of these factors created stresses which neither Taylor as an individual, nor the MEA Executive Council as a collective, could possibly bear without making a conscious effort to analyse the problems and devise positive remedies. Without this effort, conflict between Taylor and the Executive became inevitable and in the process both sides displayed the very weaknesses which contributed to their inability to deal with the original problems as they arose.

Taylor had spent many years struggling to develop trade unionism but, ironically, his success became his failure. Conditioned by the localised nature of his own experience he came to regard the development of trade unionism as an expression of his role as an individual within that development. In the formative years this view was acceptable to union members, who felt the need for a charismatic personality to whom they could look for inspiration and leadership at a time when the forces ranged against them appeared formidable. But as the MEA became firmly established Taylor's role became to be seen by many as paternalistic – dictatorial even – and incompatible with the kind of democratic procedures needed to direct the affairs of a large trade union. Taylor was unable to adapt to the new situation that he had helped create and – in what was due more to naivety than to malice – endeavoured to continue to act as he had done in the past, regardless of the Executive or anyone else. When the final rupture came the MEA Executive was able to encapsulate Taylor's dilemma by asking members, in a statement after the Manchester conference, whether they were 'prepared to support the NEC in their effort to place the Society under the control of the members, or, are they prepared to hand over the Society to the management of one man'.

The extent of Taylor's naivety was demonstrated by his attempt to enlist the district secretaries in the power struggle between himself and the Executive. He failed to recognise that the district secretaries saw their power bases in the rapidly growing memberships of their own districts, and not in a remote head office in London. And he failed to recognise that as the union expanded in size and geographical spread the district secretaries had a vested interest in the devolution of power – away from London and into the districts. Taylor's failure to discern these changes led to his conflict with some of the district secretaries and it was out of this that an alliance arose between the district secretaries and Executive members, who had parallel interests in devolving power to the districts.

On the other hand, Taylor did understand that the expansion of the MEA would generate increasing tension between it and the more established unions, particularly the general unions. His tactics at the 1906 TUC, for example, may have been crude, unnecessarily provocative and, in the final analysis, counter-productive. But to believe, as did the MEA Executive, that the TUC resolution attacking the MEA could have been met 'by sound argument' was an equally mistaken tactic and one which showed that the reality of the situation had eluded the Executive. This was demonstrated when – three years after Taylor's break with the union – the MEA was excluded from TUC membership, despite a plea from the Executive that having got rid of Taylor the MEA should be considered as having purged itself. What the MEA Executive failed to recognise – but which Taylor did see – was that the very existence of the MEA was sufficient a threat to the general unions to provoke their hostility. If the MEA was to continue to expand there would be a corresponding growth in hostility as the general unions moved to protect their membership interests, existing and potential.

The charge by the NEC that Taylor was incapable of discharging the duties of the chief executive officer of a large and growing union throws light on another aspect of the problems that were facing the MEA. The arbitration committee ruling in Taylor's favour absolved him of any general charge of incompetence. This, however, need not have been incompatible with a situation where the demands on Taylor were so great that he found it difficult to combine his organisational duties in the field with the administrative duties at head office – where resources had not grown in step with the expansion of the union. The possibility that such a situation existed is indicated by the Executive's complaint that Taylor had an 'expensive habit of visiting branches in various parts of the country without being asked to do so'. Taylor, when confronted with conflicting demands between fieldwork and paperwork would instinctively have given priority to the fieldwork; his years as a one-man-band organiser would have ensured that. On the other hand the NEC, anxious to establish and assert its own role, would have preferred Taylor to spend his time at head office attending to general administration – leaving Executive members and district secretaries the job of establishing direct relationships with branches. Viewed from this angle it is easy to see how, in the heat of the dispute between Taylor and the Executive, a problem which arose from the historical development of the union could have become transformed into personal charge of incompetence against Taylor.

Whatever the conjecture there is no doubt that the whole dispute became extremely acrimonious and highly per-sonalised, with the protagonists descending to low levels of argument. At one point, for example, it was claimed that Davies had said that Taylor's name 'stank in the nostrils of nearly all leaders in the trade union movement'. To counter this Taylor collected testimonials from an impressive list of labour movement notables, including Kier Hardie, Charles Bowerman, Will Crooks and Will Steadman – four MPs with strong trade union connections. But Taylor did not let the matter rest there; he made the counter-allegation that the records of Davies and Tevenan with their previous unions were so bad that when it became known that they had been appointed full-time MEA officers 'hostility began to show itself' from other unions.

Charge and counter-charge of this kind were, however, only

the verbal dressing on the real issues in dispute. These were issues which originated in the extraordinary development of the union and which could have been resolved in a positive fashion had those most deeply involved been prepared to put individual considerations to one side. Instead Taylor, who – for all his short-comings – had played a key role in establishing the MEA as a national union with a promising future, was dismissed from his office as general secretary by a vote of eleven to ten. This vote split the union apart at the very time it needed its maximum strength.

NOTES

1. This account is based on MEA Executive Council Minutes, Taylor's correspondence and subsequent publications issued by Taylor and the MEA, most importantly: *My Suspension*, June 1907; *An Exposure*, NUCW 1908; *Report on Suspension of General Secretary*, MEA. There seems to have been no press coverage of the dispute.

9   A New Beginning

In one sense the establishment of the National Union of Corporation Workers in 1907 represented a turning-back of the clock because, like the pioneering unions of municipal workers some thirty years earlier, its membership was confined largely to the London area. The first quarterly report of the NUCW, published three months after the formation of the union, listed income from 42 branches of which 38 were in London or areas immediately adjacent to it. Inside London itself the union's strength was centred on employees of the London County Council, who were organised in 17 branches covering workers in the tramways, asylums, drainage services, parks and the fire brigade.

It was, therefore, the London branches which provided the foundations of the new union, and it was natural that the new leadership emerged from those branches. The formal expression of that leadership was a new style Executive Council which, directly reflecting the composition of the London membership, was elected on the basis of occupational groups in order to ensure that members in each of the services had direct representation on the central body of the union. Thus the borough council workers held five seats, the tramway, asylum and water workers two seats each, and the sewage workers and the fire brigade one seat each.

Not surprisingly, this new Executive included a number of men who had been prominent in the MEA. Jim Bradley, a park keeper and secretary of the Bethnal Green branch, had been a member of the MEA executive and Tom McGrath, from St Marylebone, had been a long standing and well respected MEA branch secretary; both were to play prominent roles in the new union. Nathaniel Green – an old friend of Taylor from West Ham – became a trustee of the new union and thus he and Taylor provided the Corporation Workers with a direct link to the days of the Vestry

Attendants helping inmates at Long Grove LCC Asylum, 1910

Employees' Union in the 1890s and the pioneering days of municipal workers' trade unionism.

Recognising the need for the infant union to consolidate its initial fragile base in order to survive and expand, the new Executive Council took, as one of its earliest decisions, the bold step of employing a second full-time officer to assist Taylor. The man appointed was Henry Bye, a socialist from Edmonton in North London. His job was to act as NUCW organiser in the capital, presumably in order to leave Taylor free to operate on a broader scale. For his part Taylor pursued the twin objectives of reinforcing the commitment of existing members to the new union while extending its activities to new areas. Seeing the MEA as the major source for immediate recruitment, Taylor mounted a constant propaganda campaign against that union. In particular he personalised the campaign by denouncing the MEA for the way it had treated him and followed this with an appeal to MEA members to quit that organisation and join their old colleagues in the new union.

The campaign was not without success and by March 1908, a year after its formation, the NUCW was able to record a tally of 58 branches. Ten of these were outside the London area, with the farthest flung being at Aberavon in Wales – the first record of the new union's activity outside England. One of the major achievements in the campaign to win over MEA members occurred in Bristol, where two sizeable MEA branches seceded to the Corporation Workers and within a short time NUCW membership in that city grew to 700, distributed in four branches. Encouraged by this expansion the Bristol members, in the summer of 1908, asked the Executive Council to provide full-time organising assistance in their city. Initially the EC rejected this request but the Bristol branches, doubtless confident of their importance to the development of the NUCW, threatened to return to the MEA unless their request was met; the EC promptly changed its mind and agreed to pay the wages for an organiser to work three days a week in Bristol. The Bristol branches accepted this arrangement and proposed that Alfred Ellery, a well known Independent Labour Party member of the Bristol City Council, be appointed to the post.[1] The appointment was made in July 1908 and Ellery became the NUCW Western

Long Grove LCC Asylum laundry, 1910

District Organiser at a wage of £1 a week, the union's first full-time worker outside London.

Inevitably, the MEA responded to the constant attacks on its membership by mounting an aggressive counter-offensive against the NUCW. This reached a high point in July 1908 when, in what turned out to be a test case, the MEA took the Woolwich branch of the NUCW to the High Court for alleged disposal of MEA funds against the rules of that union – the Woolwich branch having been one of the original MEA branches to secede and to help establish the NUCW.[2] But the court ruling failed to provide the MEA with the legal precedent it needed to prevent further losses of members and branches to the Corporation Workers; Henry Bye, in the NUCW Quarterly Report of June 1908, declared with obvious delight that the legal action had been 'a financial as well as a moral failure to the MEA'.

The continuing divisions and hostilities between the MEA and the NUCW came at a very inopportune time for municipal workers as a whole because it weakened their ability to resist the attacks on their wages and conditions which followed Conservative landslide victories in the 1906 London Borough Council elections and the London County Council elections in the following year.

The Conservatives, who had previously hidden behind the description of Moderates in London local elections, adopted the new title of Municipal Reformers and conducted a strong campaign against what they claimed was the financial extravagance of the Progressive-controlled authorities. Under this new banner they took power in every London borough with the exceptions of Bethnal Green and Battersea, a development which represented a strong set-back for the Corporation Workers' policy of relying on the ballot box to win improvements in the pay and conditions of local authority workers.

This reverse, incidentally, was reinforced three years later when the Municipal Reformers again triumphed in the London borough elections, prompting a bitter comment from London organiser Henry Bye in the NUCW Quarterly Report of September 1909. He summarised the frustration which must have been felt in the union when the electorate failed to respond in a way which was essential to the union's bargaining strategy:

The Borough Council elections have come and gone, and London has once again displayed its proverbial apathy by placing the power of administration in the hands of the master class, and the workers, either by vote, or their abstinence from voting, have ensured for themselves a continuance of slums reeking with disease and death, impure and polluted milk supplies, hungry and starved children attending your schools, unemployment intensified and low wages for municipal workers with sweated contract labour, this is too big a price to pay for the apathy of London workers, and the work of agitation, education and organisation must be pursued with greater effort than ever, until the workers recognise that they must organise themselves in a party prepared to fight for the demolition of a system of society which enables a few parasites to live on the industry of those they enslave.

If the 1906 borough council elections in London brought dismay to the NUCW it could find no solace the following year when the LCC elections swept the Municipal Reformers into power with an impressive majority of 40 seats. Unions had always found the LCC a difficult employer to deal with, even while it had been under Progressive control for the first eighteen years of its existence and had continually boasted that it was a 'model employer' which set an example to other London local authorities. In truth, as has been shown, in some respects the LCC had lagged far behind a number of other authorities in London in the way it treated its unskilled manual workers. But after the 1907 LCC elections the situation became very much worse, with the new Municipal Reform majority firmly determined to reverse any advantages that the unions may have managed to gain from the old Progressive-controlled authority. One of their early targets was the LCC Works Department and they commissioned an enquiry into its operations in the hopes that the findings would produce sufficient evidence to justify its closure. When, however, the commission gave the Works Department a clean bill of health the Municipal Reform majority simply ignored its findings and proceeded to run the department down until finally abolishing it at the end of 1909.

The LCC persisted with its refusal to establish the 30 shilling minimum weekly wage despite constant arguments by the Corporation Workers that the LCC was lagging behind other London councils on pay levels. Repeated attempts by Labour stalwarts on the council, notably Frank Smith, to secure the minimum wage were voted down with depressing regularity by the Municipal Reform majority.[3] Nor did attempts to secure holidays with pay serve any better; only the tramway workers and employees in the fire brigade workshops enjoyed this condition of employment.[4] In the fire brigade itself the LCC repeatedly refused recognition, and therefore negotiation rights, to NUCW members on the grounds that the intervention of an outside organisation – such as a trade union – between individual firemen and their superior officers would constitute a 'serious breach of discipline'.[5]

The protests by the NUCW against the LCC policies were joined by other unions through demonstrations organised by the London Trades Council. When a Bill was proposed which threatened to replace the borough councils, boards of guardians and the water and asylum boards with an enlarged LCC the NUCW was quick to see the dangerous implications for the pay and conditions of municipal workers. At one protest meeting Taylor drew a parallel between the proposals in the new Bill and what had happened when the LCC took over from the Metropolitan Board of Works in 1889, 'when the first thing it did was to impose new and harsher conditions on municipal workers and attempt unsuccessfully to deprive them of their pensions'.[6] Taylor said that the NUCW would not let this happen again, and he appealed to local authorities to meet the union's proposals for a minimum wage.

In reality, however, during this period London employers were much more likely to rescind existing minimum wage clauses than respond to union calls for their extension. In Henry Bye's home town of Edmonton, for example, the council abolished its 30 shilling minimum wage in 1908 and in Chelsea the council pushed through a series of draconian measures which reduced the status of its workers from weekly to hourly paid employees, gave foremen the right to hire and fire, and put paving work out to private contractors.[7] A campaign against the Chelsea council gathered considerable public support, and resolutions backing the workers were presented to the council from a number of public meetings. At one of these meetings Bye attacked the Chelsea councillors by describing them as 'retrogressive humbugs' who 'begrudged

Lambeth Council workers, 1907

paying their men 6d an hour for sweeping dung from under their very noses'. And he followed this up by alleging that some councillors 'could spend more in one day on champagne than a workman could spend in months'.[8] But the Chelsea councillors were unmoved by these attacks, preferring to listen to the local newspaper which urged them to stick to their guns and to resist 'agitators from beyond our borders', and they refused even to meet a deputation from the NUCW to discuss the matter.[9]

It was not only the councils controlled by the Municipal Reform groups which caused problems for the Corporation Workers; Progressive-controlled councils also cut back on workers' conditions, such as Bethnal Green which in 1907 cut one day's work in every fortnight.[10] Confronted by such a situation the NUCW concentrated its opposition on lobbying and public campaigning to secure a reversal of council decisions; it did not encourage or support industrial action. Henry Bye made this clear when he discussed the situation in Bethnal Green in the NUCW Quarterly Report of December 1907:

> I was surprised to learn that it was rumoured that we had incited men to strike against this loss of work ... No friends, nothing was further from our thoughts. We have no desire to intensify the sufferings of our members. We desire to prevent the recurrence of such inequalities by going into deeper ground, and when workers recognise the cause of these cuts the effects will be remedied, until then we must plod on with our work of organisation.

In saying this Bye was obviously restating the attitude which the Corporation Workers had inherited from the MEA and, before that, from the Vestry Employees' Union: that strikes were counter-productive and that the members' money and energy could be better spent on striking at their employers through the ballot box. But this approach was all too often non-productive. For example, in 1909 – in an attempt to stem the wage cutting which was then taking place – the NUCW decided to organise a conference of borough councils and union representatives to establish uniform wages and conditions throughout the London local authorities. The effort was a complete failure because the borough councils simply refused to take part in such a conference.[11]

The union's tactics of bringing public pressure to bear on councils were more successful, however, when used against two councils which – as part of their drive to reduce the rates and thus prove the value of Municipal Reform policies – resurrected the spectre of private contracting.

In the middle class London suburb of Lewisham a council decision to put house refuse collection, scavenging and road watering out to private contract was reversed after a campaign by the Corporation Workers which culminated in a protest of 3,000 people outside the town hall. During the campaign the union succeeded in winning a broad alliance in defence of direct labour and this proved influential enough to force the council to change its mind. A correspondent to the local newspaper voiced the opinion that the council was considering a 'cheap and nasty option' and used precisely the same arguments against private contractors that had been used by opponents of the system a decade earlier. The correspondent argued that a decision to use private contractors would mean that the ratepayer would be 'irritated and disgusted ... at the sight of his overflowing and odoriferous dustbin long overdue to be cleaned and similarly affected without by ill watered and ill swept dirty roads'.[12]

In Taylor's own borough of East Ham a similar campaign was necessary when in 1908, again in an attempt to reduce the rates, the council sought tenders for dust and scavenging work. The campaign was led by the NUCW, but as in Lewisham, it gained wide support from the local community. The *East Ham Echo* reported that 1,600 people were present at one ratepayers' meeting and that so many protesters were waiting to gain entrance to a council meeting that they were 'banging down the door of the public gallery'. The newspaper gave editorial support to the union and opened its columns to critics of the council's policy, such as the local resident who complained: 'No council has the right to delegate the sanitary arrangements of the borough over which they preside. It is a matter of life and death and should not be made the shuttlecock of party squabbles'.[13] The council eventually decided to change its policy and there is no doubt that the vigorous public campaign was an important factor in securing the change, but it was matched by the fact that not one of the tenders submitted for the work by private contractors was able to compete with the council's own direct labour force.

The attempt to re-establish private contracting in Lewisham and East Ham can be viewed only as a desperate attempt at economising by atavistic councillors who were swimming against the tide of public opinion, which by this time had accepted the superiority of direct labour. The need to employ local authority workers for services directly connected with public health was well-established and the advantage of extending direct labour to other areas of municipal activity was beginning to be recognised by many local authorities. This was demonstrated in a survey carried out in forty large towns in 1908 which revealed a significant extension of direct labour in work such as the construction and repair of highways and drainage systems. With few exceptions borough engineers and surveyors favoured direct labour because it gave them greater supervision of work as well as generally being more efficient and economic in operation.[14]

While the NUCW was fighting against Conservative domination of London local government the political scene nationally was dominated by the Liberal Party. It secured a massive majority in the 1906 general election and, at the same time, 29 Labour candidates won seats in Parliament with the assistance of a pact with the Liberals. Immediately following this election the Labour Representation Committee became the Labour Party, a significant development in the history of the trade union movement.

In return for their support for the Lloyd George Liberal Government the new Labour MPs were rewarded with the 1906 Trades Disputes Act, which removed the shackles placed on the unions by the 1901 Taff Vale judgement. Under this new law the unions were absolved from the responsibility of meeting damages claimed by employers to have arisen during strikes, and picketing was recognised as a legitimate right of workers who were on strike. These changes were important, not only for their practical effect on the functioning of trade unions but also because they were a positive recognition that the labour movement had become a real political influence. The Liberals saw this as a threat to their working class vote and as a consequence they were prepared to make concessions in an attempt to contain that threat. But NUCW affiliation to the newly-established and flourishing Labour Party was out of the question. Following the split between the MEA and the NUCW, the powerful general unions had successfully pursued the 1906 TUC resolution condemning trade unions which confined their membership to municipal employees and which were prepared to recruit all grades of those employees. Arising out of the TUC resolution a joint board of the TUC, Labour Party and General Federation of Trade Unions ruled that the MEA should be assimilated into one of the general unions by May 1910. In an effort to overcome this situation the MEA tried to change its rules so that it could recruit from the private sector – in effect, to become another general union. But this was rejected by a ballot vote of members and the MEA was subsequently excluded from TUC affiliation.[15] With such strong hostility to exclusive municipal workers' unions, any attempt by the NUCW to affiliate to the TUC and the Labour Party would have been instantly rejected – all the more so because the NUCW suffered the additional handicap of being a break-away organisation. Consequently the NUCW did not even apply for affiliation and, along with the MEA, it remained outside the mainstream of TUC and Labour Party activities at national level.

Despite this exclusion, the Corporation Workers continued their tradition of active electoral work and members were expected to make a special contribution to pay for these election expenses. The union issued election manifestos urging members to support candidates who had pledged support for a 30 shilling minimum wage, a 48 hour week, half pay during sickness and full pay following accidents at work, and a week's summer holiday. The union held meetings to publicise these demands at election times and donated cash to local election committees where candidates met with the union's approval.

The success of the Labour Party prompted its opponents to mount a campaign which criticised the power of unions to spend their funds in support of political activities; as the Labour Party received the bulk of its finances from the unions the objective was to weaken the organisation of the party by limiting its cash. This campaign culminated in 1908 when a

A West Ham Council worker's membership cards
over the period 1896-1911 showing the changes in union
organisation

member of the Amalgamated Society of Railway Servants, W.J. Osborne, brought a court action against his union to prevent it spending any of its funds on political activities. In 1909 the case went to the House of Lords which, in a decision which became known as the Osborne judgement, ruled that the union was not entitled to use its funds for political purposes. The practical effect of this ruling was to stop all unions using their cash to finance the Labour Party or to support union members who had been elected as MPs. The NUCW, however, was hit less hard by this judgement than were most unions because of its special levy for electoral purposes. This special levy continued to be applied after the Osborne judgment but its provisions were changed and members were carefully – and cleverly – informed that the special levy of a penny a quarter was for:

> Rules, contribution cards and other printing matter. The balance of such fund to be voted at the discretion of the Executive Council to kindred organisations for benevolent purposes, or in any other way allowed by law in promoting the interest of the working class generally.

A number of leading NUCW members played prominent roles in local politics during this period. Henry Hodges, a Bermondsey stalwart who had helped to found the Vestry Employees' Union, was re-elected to the Bermondsey Board of Guardians from 1894 until 1907. Jim Jeffrey, who represented poor law workers on the union's Executive Council, continued as an active Progressive member of the Chelsea Council and Board of Guardians. Taylor himself was elected to the East Ham Council in 1910 as an official Labour candidate. But Jim Bradley was unsuccessful in Bethnal Green in 1908 and Henry Bye narrowly failed to secure election in Edmonton in 1908 and 1910. In Bristol Alfred Ellery continued to play a prominent part in local politics as a member of the city council, but he maintained this position only by severing his connections with the NUCW in a way which all but destroyed the union's organisation in Bristol and which, quite coincidentally, helped Ernest Bevin to set out on a path which led him to become one of the most powerful figures in the labour movement.

The situation developed when, soon after Ellery's appointment as an organiser, one of the NUCW Bristol branches applied for affiliation to the local trades council. Earlier attempts to secure affiliation had been blocked by rival unions anxious to preserve their dominance in Bristol; on this occasion not only was the NUCW application again rejected but the trades council passed a resolution which said that Ellery would be repudiated as a Labour representative on the city council as long as he remained an organiser for the NUCW. Apparently Ellery gave greater priority to his position as a city councillor than to his job as NUCW organiser because, according to a report by Taylor in the union's Quarterly Report for September 1909, immediately following the trades council meeting Ellery gave notice of his resignation from the union. The parting was amicable and Taylor even suggested that the union present a testimonial to Ellery, 'as our answer to the Trades Council'.

Within weeks, however, Taylor received reports that Ellery was holding meetings of the NUCW under the auspices of another union and was prepared to take Corporation Workers' members into another union in return for a full-time post. A fierce battle to win the support of the Bristol members followed, with London NUCW organiser Henry Bye making several visits to Bristol in an attempt to counter the efforts of rival unions, supported by Ellery, to take over the Corporation Workers' organisation in the city. At the end of the struggle nearly 500 members were lost as all but one of the four NUCW branches in Bristol defected and Ellery became an organiser for the Workers' Union.

At this time Ernest Bevin, a carter and mineral water salesman, had been active in the local labour movement for some years but – strangely enough – he was not a member of a trade union. Following a dock strike in Bristol, during which employers attempted to use carters – who were unorganised – as scabs, an organiser of the Dockers' Union suggested to Bevin that he should recruit the carters into that union as their interests were closely related. But Ellery had also seen the possibility of recruiting the carters into the Workers' Union and, after several weeks of preparatory work, had called a meeting to set up a carters's branch.

Alan Bullock, in his biography of Bevin, recounts how the

meeting resulted in a confrontation between Ellery and Bevin as they argued the rival merits of the Workers' Union and the Dockers' Union as representatives of the carters.[16] After making his argument Bevin 'got up to push his way out, taking the rest of Ellery's meeting with him'. A few days later Bevin called a meeting under the auspices of the Dockers' Union at which a carters' branch was established and Bevin was elected as its chairman. Only a few months later Bevin became a full-time organiser for the Dockers' Union and embarked on a path which eventually led him to become the general secretary of the Transport and General Workers' Union and a prominent Cabinet Minister in Clement Attlee's post-war Labour Government.

This intense inter-union rivalry in Bristol was characteristic of much of the trade union scene during the early part of the twentieth century as competing unions struggled to mark out spheres of influence, and nowhere was this rivalry so intense as between the Corporation Workers and the MEA. Gains and losses were registered on both sides as membership switched between the two unions in the years immediately following the 1907 split. But the NUCW made a special point of emphasising its gains in 1909 when a sizeable branch of the MEA in Edinburgh seceded to the Corporation Workers and gave the new union its first members in Scotland.

At the end of the decade the NUCW could look back with some satisfaction on having survived its first three difficult and formative years; although confronted by aggressive employers and hostile competition from other unions it had managed to begin building a nationwide union from its original narrow London base. But Taylor and his colleagues were very much aware that with only 3,500 members the NUCW was still very much a fledgling and unless it could open up new areas of membership it would not be able to compete against the larger unions which were waiting to pick up the pieces should the NUCW show the slightest signs of beginning to fall apart.

NOTES

1. S. Bryher, 'An Account of the Labour and Socialist Movement in Bristol', *Bristol Labour Weekly*, June 1929.

2. The case of Cope v Crossingham was reported in *The Times*, 18 July 1908.
3. See LCC Minutes, 19 November 1907, for one example of this.
4. *Municipal Journal*, 5 May 1910.
5. This policy was decided while Progressives were still in control of the Council. See LCC Fire Brigade Committee Minutes, 5 April, 1906 and Full Council Minutes, 10 April 1906.
6. *Morning Advertiser*, 4 November 1907.
7. *Chelsea Mail and West Middlesex Advertiser*, 3 June 1910.
8. Ibid., 1 July 1910.
9. Ibid.
10. Bethnal Green Borough Council Minutes, 5 December 1907.
11. See for example Chelsea Borough Council Minutes, 29 September 1909.
12. *Kentish Mercury*, 17 July 1908.
13. *East Ham Echo*, 28 February; 6 March; 13 March; 3 April 1908.
14. *Municipal Journal*, 12 June 1908.
15. H.A. Clegg, op. cit., p.62.
16. A. Bullock, *The Life and Times of Ernest Bevin*, Vol 1, London, 1960, pp. 22-23.

10 Syndicalism and Industrial Unionism

The year 1910 marked the beginning of a period of widespread industrial conflict which lasted until the outbreak of the war in 1914 and which was so intense that it sent shock waves of fear throughout the upper echelons of British society. The record of working time lost in industrial disputes presents the bare statistical bones of the situation.

From the turn of the century until 1907 the average annual loss of working time due to industrial disputes was between $2\frac{1}{2}$ and 3 million working days. In 1908 the early warning of forthcoming conflict appeared when nearly 11 million working days were lost and then, after a brief lull in 1909, industrial unrest again ripped across the country. In each of the years 1910, 1911, 1913 and 1914 around 10 million working days were lost in strikes and lock-outs; in 1912 a strike of mineworkers sent the annual figure to a staggering 40 million days. This sharpening of industrial conflict coincided with the end of a period of economic depression and as business picked up the level of unemployment fell rapidly, dropping by half in 1909 alone. But despite this economic revival, real wages – which in 1910 were below what they had been ten years earlier – did not increase; prices, on the other hand, climbed steadily.

The effects of this situation on working class living standards generated an aggressive mood amongst many trade unionists. One of them was Jim Bradley, president of the NUCW, who used his presidential address to the 1912 annual conference of the union to deliver a militant and wide-ranging political message of a kind not usually heard at the rather sober gatherings of the Corporation Workers.

There is a fierce conflict going on between Capital and Labour, which is due to the increased cost of living, the lack of a corresponding improvement in wages, the vulgar display of

151

wealth by the rich, the increasing poverty and degradation of the workers, and the determined effort to break up Trade Unions, until it has become impossible for the workers to remain quiet, and has drawn the attention of the whole nation to the horrible conditions under which the workers exist. And through it all there runs a grand display of solidarity, that new-born spirit and cohesion among the different grades of workers that few people thought possible. These examples of this great spirit will teach the capitalist that the workers are not so insignificant as they have imagined them to be ... This revolt of the workers has driven the capitalist class into such a fit of alarm that is so great that they are trying various methods to kill the new born strength of the workers. The country has been subjected to martial law; troops with ball cartridges sent to all parts of the Kingdom to overawe the workers; a volunteer police force formed in which the members of the middle class have joined, and sworn to use their truncheons on the heads of the strikers. But in spite of it all the workers are not overawed, and are determined not to return to work until peace is proclaimed – a peace which must mean increased wages, shorter hours, better conditions, a greater share of life's comforts and the right of combination, or they are starved into submission.

This aggressive stance by Jim Bradley, a militant from London's East End, was in sharp contrast to the views expressed by Albin Taylor who – despite the rising tide of industrial conflict raging all around him – continued to emphasise the reliance of the NUCW on public pressure rather than industrial action. For example, when the union lodged a wage claim in Stepney in 1911 Taylor made specific reference to the fact that municipal workers had not been involved in the 'recent labour troubles in London', and he added, 'we hope that this will be appreciated in the proper light'. As editor of the NUCW Quarterly Report, Taylor took the opportunity of reproducing favourable newspaper quotations which congratulated the union on its no strike policy. The June 1912 issue, for example, carried an extensive report from the *Stratford Express* on the unveiling of a new branch banner by the mayor of East Ham, where Taylor himself was a councillor. The meeting was opened by a local councillor who was also a member of the Corporation Workers and who made the point:

In a leaflet issued some time ago by the general secretary it was shown that since the Union had been in existence the cost of improvements in the conditions of employment had amounted to £200,000 a year without a strike.

Taylor himself underlined this when he said that the new banner was 'an emblem of fraternal greeting and not of aggressive action'. As the newspaper reported: 'The banner was then unfurled by the Mayor. It bore the representation of an official of the Union paying out a funeral claim to the widow of a member.'

But in the trade union movement as a whole attention was directed on issues other than funeral benefits as one group of workers after another – railwaymen, dockers, miners, seaman, transport workers and builders – became locked into fierce disputes with employers. An influential current running through this surge of industrial activity was the concept of syndicalism as a new weapon in the hands of the workers, and its most vigorous exponent was the veteran socialist, Tom Mann. Mann's syndicalist views have been summarised by B.C. Roberts, a historian of the TUC, as follows:

The essence of Tom Mann's beliefs was that the existing trade unions were moribund. They were unable to act in a militant fashion because they had accepted the philosophy of liberal capitalism, and their organisation, based on the craft divisions of industry, was not fitted for the struggle with the capitalist owners who had improved on the example of the workers and had organised themselves on industrial lines. He advocated the creation of industrial unions, linked together in national federations, under the central direction of the General Federation of Trade Unions, which should then be affiliated to an international federation of trade unions. He urged the abandonment of collective agreements, which, he alleged, sapped the vigour of the trade unions because they bound them to the employers, thus destroying the unions' freedom to attack. Trade unions had no right to sacrifice their independence in this, he argued; all collective agreements should therefore be denounced and the employers assaulted at every opportunity by means of the strike. For tactical reasons, Tom Mann did not suggest the dissolution of the Labour Party, but he did not believe that the workers could abolish capitalism by constitutional political means; this objective could only be achieved by the use of direct

LCC employee washing down a Thames Embankment seat, circa
1910

industrial action. The workers ought, therefore, to concentrate on preparing for the revolutionary strike, and not waste their time working for reforms through a parliamentary system which only corrupted their representatives.[1]

Arising out of his energetic activities in various industrial disputes, Tom Mann was able to develop an organisation which made its presence felt in a number of industries, particularly on the railways, amongst the building workers and with the miners of South Wales.[2] But not all of Mann's allies were necessarily committed to the totality of his syndicalist philosophy. Many wanted only to reorganise the structure of the trade union movement on an industrial rather than a craft or sectional basis in order to make it a more effective instrument of collective bargaining. Others were expressing a general anti-establishment attitude, particularly in the light of the Osborne judgement and the failure of Labour MPs to secure parliamentary action to rectify the wrongs inflicted on the unions by that judgement. And many more were articulating rank and file impatience with what they considered to be the lack of a militant response by trade union and Labour Party leaders to the attacks on working class living standards.

Inevitably the supporters and opponents of such views clashed and wide divisions opened up in the working class movement. Major debates involving the policies advocated by the syndicalists and industrial unionists took place at the annual meeting of the TUC between 1910 and 1912 and one of the leading exponents of industrial unionism was a member of the Operative Bricklayers' Society, Jack Wills, who in later years was to play a significant role in the development of the Corporation Workers.

The NUCW itself – despite its lack of involvement in industrial disputes – became involved in the debate on syndicalism and industrial unionism when the issue was raised at its national conferences in the period 1911-13. The main protagonists were members of the London-based Metropolitan Water Board branch, which proposed the amalgamation of unions catering for municipal workers as a move towards industrial unionism. After ineffective and somewhat confused debates in 1911 and 1912 the Executive

Council – clearly determined that the union should not get drawn over to the militant wing of the trade union movement as represented by Tom Mann and his supporters – produced a lengthy statement on the subject for endorsement by delegates to the 1913 annual conference.

The statement, while concluding that the union should keep its options open because of the lack of evidence of any concrete advantages to the NUCW through amalgamation, produced a whole catalogue of reasons why the union should continue its separate existence and eschew industrial action as it had in the past.

Reviewing candidates for amalgamation the statement recorded that according to Board of Trade statistics there were fourteen unions of municipal workers. Eleven of these were local organisations and were dismissed by the EC with the comment, 'with these we should have to take all liabilities'. The three remaining national unions consisted of the Corporation Workers itself, the Asylum Workers and the MEA. The possibility of amalgamation which the Asylum workers was discounted in two dozen words which pointed out that its contributions were only a penny a week, that it paid no benefits and that its local officers and delegates 'carry out their duties almost voluntarily'. Having despatched twelve of the possible thirteen candidates for amalgamation, this as the EC statement commented, 'leaves us and the MEA'. Then, in bold black type, it set out the Executive's case against amalgamation with the MEA:

> In view of the spiteful litigation they have instituted against us (in which the homes of your EC Delegates the Trustees of the Woolwich Branch, and of our General Secretary was threatened to be sold) also the fact that their contributions are $\frac{1}{2}$d. per week more than ours with less benefits, the many strikes they have had, their past and present hostile attitude towards us (to show this is a fact one branch moved at one of their Conferences that amalgamation be sought with us, but no one seconded the motion) we feel that we cannot go back to them so long as they retain their present advisors.

Having thus disposed of the practical possibilities of amalgamation the EC statement continued at some length to attack the militant stance associated with the supporters of industrial unionism and to extol the virtues of the policies advocated by Taylor, long followed by the union: 'Speaking generally our members have the best conditions of employment; our relations with Local Authorities and their Officers are cordial, and every representation we make is considered and two-thirds conceded.' And it warned:

> Another consideration should not be overlooked, viz., that just as Labour perfects its organisation for aggression so Capital will follow suit, just like countries do with their armies and navies. Until force meets force, and the question will be who will get the best of the fighting, and when they are all over what then?

As if answering its own question the EC pointed out that more than 40 million working days had been lost in industrial disputes during the previous year and it calculated that this would have cost workers some £1,250,000 in lost wages. 'We prefer constant employment under tolerable conditions to such doubtful advantages,' commented the Executive, and added,

> In our opinion municipal workers have secured by far the best results so far; we claim that most of the improvements have been gained as a result of our work and policy without strikes or asking members for an extra halfpenny.

The EC statement concluded:

> Our advice and recommendation is (unless the advocates of Amalgamation can guarantee us better terms as to payments and benefits and better conditions of labour than we now have), to wait, keep an open mind on the subject, and should a favourable opportunity present itself seize the opportunity.

After again reminding members that the union had 'secured concessions costing the Local Authorities about £200,000 per annum without a strike' and cataloguing the union's financial assets it ended: 'Don't throw it away for a shadow.'

The members of the Metropolitan Water Board branch countered the EC's lengthy statement with an equally lengthy statement which made a robust defence of industrial unionism

Metropolitan Water Board workers in the Fleet sewer

and attacked what it saw as the failures of the NUCW
leadership.

After noting the moves towards union amalgamations on
the railways and in the building industry, and the activities of
amalgamation committees in most major industries, the
Water Board branch pointed to the fact that in recent strikes
capital was well-organised and was assisted by a Liberal
Government which used the police and armed forces against
the strikers. 'Whilst not wishing for or advocating strikes [we]
must recognise that this is, after all, the workers' chief
weapon.' The statement then sought, by implication, to rebut
the Executive Council's claim on the benefits that had been
won for municipal workers:

> The Local Government Act of 1888 brought into existence the
> various County Councils, since which, both parties – Moderate
> and Progressive – have both dominated the LCC, the latter most
> of the time; yet there are employed by the LCC over 4,000
> workers at less than 30s. per week. Firemen are practically always
> on duty; asylum workers hours are notoriously long, main
> drainage men seven days per week, and Tramway men speeded
> up for all they are worth.
>
> Another instance the Water Board: Men transferred from the
> old companies to the Board have their rights, etc., guaranteed
> them by Act of Parliament, yet your union has been unable even
> to obtain these for the men. If those with an Act of Parliament to
> assist them cannot win, how do the majority of workers fare
> without such.
>
> Again, whilst capital had been concentrating its forces wages
> have rapidly decreased, viz., the purchasing power of the £ today
> is only equal to 15s.6d. of seven years ago; therefore, has not the
> time arrived for us to fix our minimum at 35s. per week for a six
> hour day?

Nor did union officials, such as Taylor himself, escape
criticism by the Water Board members. Responding to EC
arguments that incompatibility between the full-time officials
of different unions created problems for amalgamations, the
Water Board branch statement commented sharply:
'Respecting officials, let us control them, not them us. Any
squabbles amongst them deal with them summarily,

especially as their wages are, more often, more for one week than some of ours are for three.'

After proposing a conference of all unions catering for municipal workers to construct a new amalgamated society, the statement concluded with a call to the class struggle which displayed the militant influence of syndicalist ideas: 'Let us link up in the coming great federation of Labour and stand shoulder to shoulder in the great impending fight, remembering – The Unity of Labour is the hope of the world.'

Couched in such terms the ideas advanced by the Water Board Branch proved too strong a mixture for delegates more accustomed to the traditional approach of the Corporation Workers. When the votes were taken the Metropolitan Water Board branch statement was rejected by twenty votes to four and a further vote of nineteen to one endorsed the position in the EC statement. The result expressed opposition to militant action and continuing hostility to the MEA rather than a rejection of the general principle: unity of municipal workers in a single union. It also demonstrated that – however sharp the industrial struggle might be in the country at large – members of the NUCW were prepared to follow the policies of moderation advocated by Taylor.

One of the factors which helped to generate industrial unrest, and at the same time prompted many trade unionists to turn to syndicalism and industrial unionism for a solution to their problems, was the continuing effect of the 1909 Osborne judgement. Although the formal effect of that judgement was to restrain the Amalgamated Society of Railway Servants from using its funds to support the Labour Party or to maintain Members of Parliament, the complex decision of the Law Lords in presenting that judgement not only extended the effects to other unions but also covered a much wider area of trade union activity than political action. In deciding that trade unions were corporate bodies formed under statute, and therefore unable to do lawfully anything outside of the purpose for which the statute had incorporated them, the Law Lords drove the activities of the unions back to the confines of the 1876 Trade Union Act – which had never been intended to serve such a purpose.

The historians Sidney and Beatrice Webb, in the second edition of their monumental history of trade unionism published eleven years after the Osborne judgement, explained the situation as follows:

> Trade unions found themselves suddenly forbidden to do anything, even if all of their members desired it, which could not be brought within the terms of a clause in the Act of 1876, which Parliament (as Lord James of Hereford emphatically declared) never meant to be taken in that sense.[3]

Not only did the terms of the Osborne judgement inhibit trade union involvement in politics it also placed at risk all of their educational work, their association for common purposes in trades councils and even their participation in the TUC.

In an attempt to pacify more moderate elements in the trade unions – and thus strengthen their hands against militant sections who were supporting the syndicalists and industrial unionists – in 1911 Parliament introduced a measure which conceded a payment of £400 a year to all MPs. But while this move eased the position of Labour MPs who had been deprived of union funds to support them in Parliament it did nothing to restore trade union rights, and as a result it did nothing to quell the rising tide of trade union agitation throughout the country. Eventually, confronted with increasing industrial unrest which frequently contained a strong element of anti-parliamentarism – and after a struggle between ministers in the cabinet itself – in 1913 the government introduced a Bill to Parliament which sought to rectify the situation created by the Osborne Judgement.

The 1913 Trade Union Act did not, however, completely restore the freedom of trade unions to engage in politics in the way they had prior to the Osborne judgement. Under the 1913 Act any trade union wishing to finance specific political objects was required to hold a ballot and, if a majority of those members voting agreed, to set up a separate political fund for those purposes. If such a fund was established any dissenting members could claim exemption from contributing to it; in other words, having lost the vote the minority could then contract out of the ballot decision.

The Executive of the Corporation Workers, having decided that it would be 'very advisable to have a representative in the House of Commons, which would secure our interest being looked after there, and add materially to our status as a Union', therefore recommended to the 1914 conference of the union that a ballot of members be held to establish a political fund under the provisions of the 1913 Act. The EC recommendation was adopted by the conference on a card vote, with 93 in favour and 45 against. A month later the ballot of members produced a majority of two to one in favour of a political fund; at the same time contributions were increased from 2½d a week to 3d and 10 per cent of contribution income was specifically designated for the political fund. But if the NUCW was back in political business within the terms of the law it was still not accepted by the Labour Party itself, as was demonstrated in 1916 when an application by the union for affiliation to the Labour Party was rejected – an inevitable decision in view of the continued exclusion of the NUCW from the ranks of the TUC.

Despite this exclusion from the national councils of the labour movement the NUCW continued to grow in size and, equally importantly, to establish itself in areas far removed from its original London base. A concerted recruitment campaign in Yorkshire and Lancashire during 1912 yielded more than 1,000 new members and respectably sized branches existed in Pontefract, Wakefield, Burnley, Rochdale and St Helens. In the East Midlands, with some 700 members, branches existed in Norwich, Peterborough, Loughborough, Chesterfield and Nottingham. There was also some recruitment in the South West, with branches operating in Reading, Exeter and Bristol. The most significant growth occurred in Edinburgh, where by 1914 the branch could claim 900 members. Meanwhile in London itself membership continued to grow, notably in Westminster where 500 council workers joined the NUCW in 1913 and amongst the firemen – where an influx of members during November and December of 1913 took the membership of the Fire Brigade branch to an impressive 1,100.

Amongst many of these newly organised members, wages and conditions were abysmal and in some places the union's claim for a 25 shilling minimum provincial area wage seemed to be an impossible objective. In Rowley Regis, Stourbridge and Rugby there were members who earned only 16 shillings a week in 1912. In Dudley the wages of street sweepers varied

Water Board workers cleaning filter beds

between 15 and 19 shillings for a 54 hour week. In the wealthy city of Edinburgh the lavatory attendants were paid only 18 shillings a week. Very few of these workers enjoyed holidays with pay, sick-pay or pension schemes. Because many of them could be dismissed without the right to appeal, victimisation occurred as they began to organise themselves in the NUCW.[4]

In London, the stronghold of the union, the majority of the borough councils and other public authorities continued to refuse to recognise the 30 shilling minimum weekly wage, which still remained the union's objective despite the fact that it had been eroded by inflation of nine per cent between 1909 and 1913. One estimate of the weekly income necessary to sustain the average working class family in 1914 was 31s 3d, a figure well above the earnings of most NUCW members, many of whom where amongst the 25 per cent of adult workers whose wages fell below the poverty line in 1914.[5]

In the London borough of Deptford the attempt to win a 30 shilling minimum in 1911 was defeated at a heated council meeting which ended in complete disorder as council workers in the gallery showed their anger over the decision.[6] In the once enlightened borough of Bermondsey new by-laws were introduced in 1911 which abolished the permanent status of hundreds of its employees, removed the special payment made to men unable to work because of the weather and put all employees under the complete control of the foremen – a move which Taylor complained in a letter to the council could 'do incalculable harm with such wide discretion'. The council even went so far as to pass a by-law which threatened with dismissal any employee who discussed 'public questions' with fellow employees.[7]

The Metropolitan Water Board was also proving to be a problem for the Corporation Workers. During 1912 and 1913 the union conducted an effective recruitment campaign amongst Water Board employees who looked forward to action by the union to settle grievances which had existed – and grown – since the Board had taken over from the private companies in 1902. The union was able to demonstrate that the conditions of some of the workers were worse than they had been before 1902; it protested that the 25 shilling minimum wage being paid was inadequate and should be raised to 30 shillings with a basic 48 hour week. But the Board refused to receive any representations from the NUCW, instead it consulted a staff association which the NUCW said was more interested with 'soft jobs and promotions' than with the real interests of the employees. Despite these difficulties improvements were made in 1913 and 1914 to bring the minimum wage up to 28 shillings.[8] These gains owed more to the concerted agitation of the Corporation Workers – which by this time represented nearly one-third of the 3,000 waged workers – than they did to the staff association, which Taylor said did nothing but mouth 'servile and lickspittle expressions'.

Problems of recognition also faced the Fire Brigade branch, which following its rapid growth at the end of 1913 was able to claim that it represented the overwhelming majority of London's full-time firemen. This did not, however, impress the LCC, which had stood resolutely against union recognition for firemen since it was first approached by the MEA in 1905. In November 1913 the chief officer advised the LCC Fire Brigade Committee to stamp hard on union agitation for recognition by sacking the NUCW branch secretary, E.W. Southgate and it was probably an attempt to avert this threat which prompted the union to nominate Executive Council member Jim Bradley as a replacement branch secretary.[9] Bradley clearly empathised with the firemen because, though not a fireman himself, he was the son of a London fireman and had, in fact, been born in a fire station in 1867.[10] In an attempt to quell this developing trade unionism the LCC offered the firemen a staff committee through which they could raise their grievances, but this was unacceptable to the firemen who insisted that their affairs be dealt with through the union. The LCC, however, was determined to have nothing to do with the NUCW and in July 1914 the Fire Brigade Committee, by a vote of seven to five, rejected the firemen's demand along with claims for increased pay, one day off in seven, better pensions, and improvements for families who lived in fire brigade quarters. The real sticking point was the question of union representation, and on this neither side was prepared to give way. Even the Government's Chief Industrial Commissioner, Sir George Askwith, was unable to find common ground when asked to intervene.[11]

By 1914 membership of the NUCW had grown to nearly 8,500, having more than doubled since 1911. While this growth had put the union on a sound organisational and financial footing it was still vulnerable to competition from other unions, as evidenced by the fact that the MEA had also doubled its membership over the same period to reach a total of 25,000.

With the geographical spread of this increased membership the system of election to the NUCW Executive Council, devised in 1907 and based on London's predominance at that time, proved to be unsatisfactory in providing adequate representation for the newly recruited members in the provinces. In 1912, for example, there was no contest for the Executive seats for Asylums, Water Board, Tramways, Poor Law and Fire Brigade sections but fierce competition for the six borough council seats. In 1913 London members held twelve of the fourteen seats on the Executive. Branches outside London obviously considered the situation to be unfair and unjustified and at the 1914 conference the branches from St Helens and Crewe proposed a new system of election based on the grouping of branches throughout the country into electoral divisions, with each division having the power to elect one EC member for every one-thirteenth of the full membership. This new system was endorsed by conference delegates on a card vote by the narrow majority of 70 votes to 67.

At the same conference the same two branches proposed another successful alteration to the rules which demonstrated quite clearly, despite rumblings from the syndicalists in earlier debates, that Taylor was the man at the top. A member of the Executive with full voting rights, Taylor was – according to rule – subject to periodic elections; he had in fact been challenged only once, in 1912 when he defeated his opponent by 101 votes to 4. The 1914 conference changed this when, in the words of the resolution to remove 'the anxiety of re-election', he was made a permanent official with no need to submit himself to further elections.

When delegates left the Bell Hotel in London's Old Bailey on Whit Monday 1914 there was no thought in their minds that before the next conference met a year later, many of them would be involved in battles of a very different kind.

NOTES

1. B.C. Roberts, *The Trade Union Congress 1868-1921*, London, 1958, p.237.
2. B. Holton, *British Syndicalism 1910-1914*, London, 1976.
3. S. and B. Webb, *History of Trade Unionism*, London, 1920, p.610.
4. *Municipal Journal*, 13 September 1912.
5. A.L. Bowley, *Wages and Income in the U.K. since 1860*, London, 1937, p.31.
   G.K. Burgess, *The Challenge of Labour*, London, 1980, p.115.
6. *Kentish Mercury*, 26 May 1911.
7. Bermondsey Borough Council Minutes, 21 November 1911.
8. Metropolitan Water Board Minutes, 7 March 1913; 1 May 1914.
9. LCC Fire Brigade Committee Minutes, 27 November 1913.
10. F. Radford, *Fetch the Engine*, London 1951, pp. 86-93.
11. LCC Fire Brigade Committee Minutes, 5 February 1914.

11   A War Within a War

As the war clouds gathered in Europe during the summer of 1914 most trade unionists, in common with the remainder of the population, gave little thought to the possibility that Britain would soon become involved in a bloody conflict which would ultimately embrace all of the major world powers and cost millions of lives. The attention of trade unionists was turned inwards, towards a turbulent domestic scene where one union after another was becoming involved in bitter industrial disputes, which in the first half of 1914 were breaking out at a rate of something like 150 a month. Describing this period in their *History of Trade Unionism*, Sidney and Beatrice Webb wrote: 'British Trade Unionism was, in fact, in the summer of 1914, working up for an almost revolutionary outburst of gigantic industrial disputes.'[1]

In so far as they were concerned with international affairs, trade unions shared the general view of the labour movement that Britain should not become involved in any dispute between Serbia and Austria except to play the part of a peacemaker, and they placed great reliance on the ability of the strong alliance of German trade unionists and social democrats to contain the conflict by preventing their government from taking sides. However, when Germany entered into the war the anti-militarist stance of the working class movement in that country collapsed and this provoked a similar rapid change in the attitudes of the British labour movement. Two days before Britain's entry into the war on 4 August, massive demonstrations were held in London and other major towns and cities where leaders of the labour movement urged opposition to militarism and their enthusiastic supporters passed resolutions calling on the government to refrain from any involvement in the war. But less than a week later the anti-war leader of the Parliamentary Labour Party, Ramsay MacDonald, had resigned and been replaced

CORPORATION WORKERS,

Nat. Tel., Ilford 127   *Registered No., 1386 T.U.*

Offices : 138, FIRST AVENUE, MANOR PARK, LONDON, E.

Secretary, Councillor A. TAYLOR.

Grave Unrest among the London Firemen.

Concessions which cost but little granted, the real and substantial ones deferred, viz. :—
Increase in wages ; one day's rest in seven ; and earlier pensions.
Men refused a Conciliation Board or a Society to voice their greivances.

A MASS MEETING

WILL TAKE PLACE ON

MONDAY, FEB. 22nd, 1915,

4 P.M., AT

Carr's Restaurant, Strand, W.C.

Mr. T. McGRATH, President of Union,

WILL PRESIDE. Supported by

A. W. YEO, M.P., J.P., L.C.C.,

The Officers and Committee of the Branch, and Councillor A. TAYLOR, Secretary.

Members of the L.C.C. and general public cordially invited.

The following Members of Parliament regret their inability to be present, but wish the Firemen of London every success in their fight for justice :—
Percy Alden, M.P., Sir J. H. Bethell, Bart., M.P., C. W. Bowerman, M.P., H. G. Chancellor, M.P., Will Crooks, M.P., G. Roberts, M.P., J. P. Nanetti, M.P., and S. Walsh, M.P.

F. W. SCRASE, Printer [T.U.] 151, Barking Road, London, E.   *P.T.O.*

Corporation workers' handbill supporting London firemen

by Arthur Henderson, an MP with his roots in the iron founders' union. This was a sign that – whatever they may have said a few days before – the leaders of the labour movement were already committed to supporting the war. The formal confirmation of this position took place on 24 August when the Joint Board – a body which represented the TUC, the Labour Party and the General Federation of Trade Unions – met and agreed that all unions should take immediate steps to end existing disputes and urged that for the duration of the war every effort should be made to settle differences between workers and employers without resorting to stoppages of work. A few months later, in March 1915, at a meeting resided over by Chancellor of the Exchequer Lloyd George, representatives of the TUC and the major individual unions signed a document, known as the Treasury Agreement, which set a new pattern for government-union relations. Under this agreement the unions accepted – amongst other things – that they would forgo the use of strikes for the duration of the war, that unresolved disputes would be referred to arbitration and that union restrictive practices would be relaxed subject to certain safeguards. In the event this agreement failed to produce the results the government expected and it was later superseded by more stringent measures; but the fact that union leaders were prepared to commit themselves to the Treasury Agreement was an important indication of the extent to which they were prepared to support the war.

Notwithstanding the readiness of the unions to support the war effort at national level, which was reinforced when Labour MPs joined a coalition government in May 1915, industrial relations were a source of continual trouble. With prices and profits rising and unions at national level constrained from taking strike action, rank and file dissidents – in some cases remnants of the syndicalist and industrial union movement – combined to create shop stewards' committees and to lead localised strikes. When the particular disputes were settled these rank and file organisations often remained in existence and were later to provide a base for significant developments in the pattern of British trade unionism.

The National Union of Corporation Workers, given its size

Burst water main at Ealing Common, 1916

and the nature of the work its members performed, did not feature largely in trade union history during these wartime years. But the evidence that does exist shows that the NUCW and its members experienced problems similar to those of workers in the industries which, because of their importance to war production, received most public attention.

For example, to offset the impact of the continually rising cost of living – which doubled in the years between 1914 and 1918 – the NUCW devoted much of its energy to negotiating war bonuses with individual employing authorities. However, the Local Government Board was urging local authorities to abolish wasteful spending as a contribution to the war effort and some councils actually used this exhortation to reject the union's applications for war bonuses.[2]

The contrast between the parsimonious attitude of some local authorities in resisting the union's efforts to protect members from rising prices, and the rich pickings that were being made from the war by some sections of the population caused considerable resentment amongst the union's members. The union's President, Walter Conquer, articulated this resentment when he gave his presidential address to the union's 1917 national conference. After expressing regret at the continuation of the war, which was 'causing untold misery and desolation to numbers of our fellow workers and comrades', he asked: 'When will this terrible slaughter cease?' He continued to answer his own question:

> Not while the diplomats quarrel about who will be top dog; not while food profiteers can make their pile out of the food of the people ... not while the employers can make such large profits on war work; not while shipping companies can make such enormous sums of money that they hardly know what to do with it; not while nations crave for more power and dominion. No! The People, The Workers, the blood, bone and sinew of the Nations – the Workers – they are the ones who will end this massacre.

The strong condemnation by Conquer of food profiteers was underlined when the conference delegates attacked the inaction of the government Food Controller, Lord Davenport, which they said was allowing the public to be 'systematically

robbed by the Profiteers'; they demanded that Lord
Davenport be removed from office immediately – 'or asked to
resign'.

The frustration felt by NUCW members grew as the war
continued, and it was marked by a change of the union's
attitude towards the use of the strike weapon, as its claims for
war bonus payments to meet the steady upwards spiral of
price increases were resisted by employing authorities. The
real crunch came on April 1918 when the union was faced
with resistance from a number of councils in London who
refused to make any offer in response to a union claim for a £1
a week war bonus. Determined to force the issue after
repeated attempts to make progress had failed, the union gave
the offending councils a deadline of 10 August by which to
make wage improvements. If the councils failed to respond by
this date the members were given authority to take strike
action in support of the claim. Faced with this ultimatum,
which they recognised as a determined display of the
NUCW's newly-found militancy, five councils rapidly
conceded the full £1 claimed by the union and a number of
others followed with offers which the members found
acceptable.[3] By 14 September it was reported to the Executive
Council that only Holborn council was holding out and had
failed to make a satisfactory offer; the Executive responded by
calling upon the Holborn members to take immediate strike
action. The call met with a complete walk out by the
members.

After the strike had been in progress for a week the council
made its first attempt at strike-breaking by recruiting a group
of women to work as street cleaners. Five women carrying
brooms left the council depot accompanied by the
superintendent. But, as the local newspaper reported, the
strike-breaking attempt suffered immediate defeat. The
strikebreakers, said the newspaper,

had hardly got into the main thoroughfare when a number of women
immediately set upon them and took possession of their brooms. The
five women took to flight and made for the yard again pursued by
the women relatives or wives of the men on strike ... One woman
declared that the wives were determined not to allow any women
street cleaners to replace their husbands.[4]

At its meeting two days later the council agreed to discuss wages with the workers, but only as individuals and not through the union. The council said that if the strikers did not accept this procedure the matter would be dealt with by 'contracting outside for the cleaning of the streets'.[5] The 110 strikers refused to accept the council's ultimatum and decided to do battle with the blacklegs. The contractors were duly hired but, as a report to the council a month later recorded, they 'found it impossible to carry out the work in consequence of our inability to obtain proper police protection against the strikers'. Confronted with this determined display of union resistance the council capitulated and agreed to meet the claim for the £1 war bonus.[6]

Although the main weight of the NUCW's strength was centred in London its extended organisation meant that it was able to flex its muscles in other parts of the country. In the Yorkshire town of Pontefract, for example, the members also came out on strike in September 1918 against the refusal of the council to pay a war bonus. Initially the council responded in a belligerent fashion and accused the strikers of laziness and of destroying the good relationship that had existed between the council and its employees in the past. The workers, however, continued to give solid support to the strike and eventually the council was forced to agree that the issue went to arbitration, which found totally in the workers' favour.[7]

This determination to use the strike weapon if employing authorities failed to respond to union claims communicated itself to the London firemen, who had been encouraged by Taylor to act in the interest of public safety during the war and not pursue their claim for union recognition. But by the autumn of 1918, embracing the mood of militant action, the firemen decided that the time had come to once again press their demand; it was a decision which was to have unexpected consequences for the NUCW.

The mood of the firemen was militant and they were determined to take action if no concessions were made. The London *Evening Standard* reported their secretary Jim Bradley as saying that the firemen were 'fed up with flattery and petty tyranny', and he warned that although strike action would involve a major breach of discipline, 'I do not think that will deter the men.'[8] This determination confronted the London

County Council's chief fire officer, Lt Commander Sladen, when he addressed a representative body of the firemen. According to a report in *The Star* on 7 September 1918, the firemen told their chief officer that they would stand by the union and, 'if the Executive tell us to "down tools" we will down them immediately'.[9]

Neither side was prepared to give way and as the union held a strike ballot of the firemen the Government's Chief Industrial Commissioner, Sir George Askwith, intervened and held meetings with the NUCW Executive and the Fire Brigade Committee of the LCC. Jim Bradley acted as the spokesman for the fireman and he reiterated their demands for union recognition with the right of the firemen to choose an outsider as their secretary if they wished. He added that the firemen also wanted significant improvements in pay and conditions. One point, which the LCC had consistently raised, was cleared up by Bradley when he gave an assurance that the Fire Brigade branch of the union would not become involved in labour disputes outside the fire service or outside London. In making this statement Bradley undermined one of the major arguments used by the council when resisting union recognition for the firemen. This was that if London firemen belonged to a national union with members in all council services they could be called on to take action in support of workers who were involved in a dispute that had nothing to do with the London Fire Service. Bradley declared that this would not happen as the branch enjoyed complete autonomy; 'No other action of the Union has anything to do with the Fire Brigade Branch,' he said. This statement was not accepted by the council, but it appeared to have an impact on Sir George Askwith who extended the proposition by questioning Bradley about the possibility of the firemen forming their own union. The LCC spokesman, Mr G.H. Hume, took advantage of the opening made by Askwith by implying that the council would be much more sympathetic to the firemen's demands if they belonged to a separate union. Bradley replied by saying:

What the Gentleman wants is for us to leave our union which we have built up and we do not intend to do so,' and then he added a qualification, 'unless we see some very good reasons why we should throw it over.[10]

The outcome of this initial meeting was an offer by the LCC Fire Brigade Committee to submit the matter to arbitration; this offer was accepted by the union and the date for the hearing was fixed as 18 September.

When the hearing opened it was clear that the idea of recognition being conceded to an independent firemen's trade union was firmly established in the minds of the main participants. For the LCC, Hume accepted 'the principle of a trade union in the Brigade', and said what the council was fighting was 'a larger union with interests outside'. When Bradley asked if an independent firemen's union with an outsider as its secretary would be acceptable to the council, Hume said that it would. Given these kind of exchanges it was almost a foregone conclusion that when the arbitration decision was published on 23 September, Askwith recommended that the LCC should establish a representative body through which grievances could be channelled and that it should recognise a London Fire Brigade Union, the spokesman of which need not be a member of the fire brigade.[11]

Up to this point all negotiations on behalf of the NUCW had been conducted by Bradley, the Executive Council having decided to leave the matter in the hands of the Fire Brigade branch and to await the outcome of the arbitration. However, when the arbitration award was made and the possibility that the union would lose the members of the Fire Brigade branch became a real threat, Taylor immediately involved himself in the matter. After letters to Askwith asking for an explanation of the award, Taylor paid a personal visit to Askwith's office to express concern that the union could lose 1,000 members as a result of the award. The civil servant who received Taylor noted that he had the distinct impression that, 'the feeling between his Union and the Firemen's Branch was somewhat strained at the present'.[12] Meanwhile, Bradley was apparently preparing the way for the secession of the Fire Brigade branch into the small Firemen's Trade Union; without consulting Taylor or the NUCW executive he called a meeting on 31 March 1919, at which the branch officially left the NUCW and joined the Firemen's Trade Union. A week later the NUCW executive condemned Bradley for behaviour 'against the interests of the Union', deprived the Fire Brigade branch members of benefit rights and issued an order for the return of all NUCW property.

It is clear, therefore, that this was no parting of the ways by mutual consent but was a serious split in the ranks of the NUCW, and the personal animosity between Bradley and Taylor spilled over into a libel case before the Lord Chief Justice in November 1919.[13] The case arose when an Edinburgh fireman wrote to Bradley, in his new capacity as assistant general secretary of the Firemen's Trade Union, asking for details of that organisation. In his reply Bradley was foolish enough to state that one of the reasons why the London firemen had broken away from the NUCW was Taylor's incompetence in dealing with fire brigade issues and that he had deliberately underplayed the firemen's efforts to improve their conditions. This letter was apparently passed to Taylor who – having considerable experience in this kind of business – decided to take the matter to the courts. On the day of the hearing Bradley admitted responsibility, withdrew the allegations and agreed to pay £100 legal costs. The NUCW report for 1920, written by Taylor himself, recorded with a great deal of self-satisfaction: 'In this Mr Taylor has not been vindictive. He could have driven his claims right home for damages to himself. He is not of that spirit, his life having been spent on trying to do good not harm.'

The loss of more than 1,000 members from its ranks was undoubtedly a severe blow to the finances of the Corporation Workers and, equally important, its aspirations to represent all grades of municipal workers. But the secession of the firemen became almost inevitable once Askwith and the LCC floated the possibility of recognition on condition that the firemen broke away from the NUCW. The links between the firemen's branch and the rest of the union had never been strong; the branch operated in an autonomous fashion and the rank and file firemen, although becoming increasingly class conscious, considered themselves as a distinct group with particular needs and did not feel any great sense of loyalty to other municipal workers. They were therefore prepared to quit the NUCW and become an independent union in order to achieve recognition from the employer. For its part, the Executive of the Corporation Workers complained that Bradley had not given Taylor the opportunity to put the union's position to the firemen after the Askwith arbitration award, and Bradley certainly acted in an underhand manner in not informing Taylor of meetings at which firemen considered the future of the branch. On the other hand, it is difficult to think of anything Taylor or anyone else could have done which would have convinced the firemen to stay with NUCW with the prospect of a strike for recognition when they had effectively already secured acceptable recognition.

While the new-found militancy that arose in the NUCW during the war years was important to the development of the union itself it was of minor significance when set alongside the growing unrest in many industrial centres. Many rank and file trade unionists in the production industries were frustrated by the restrictive wartime legislation which inhibited union activity and the involvement of their national unions in the operation of that legislation. As a consequence they turned to 'unofficial' action to secure a settlement of their grievances. Through this process the shop stewards – who initially were little more than recruiting agents and dues collectors – emerged as local union negotiators who acted as the focal point for discontent and became the natural leaders of workers in strike situations. In some industries, principally engineering, the shop stewards developed national and district organisations which became militant alternative power bases outside the formal union structure. The wartime strikes were therefore much more than an immediate problem which disrupted the war effort, they were also indicators of fundamental changes in power relationships taking place within the unions and, consequently, in the institutionalised arrangements for negotiations between unions and employers and between unions and government. Union leaders, employers and government therefore began to look for corrective action which would halt these developments by minimising conflict and stabilising the industrial scene on a long-term basis.

The views of the union leaders were set out by Harry Gosling, general secretary of the Lightermen's Union, in his presidential address to the TUC in 1916. In what amounted to a direct appeal to employers for a combined operation, Gosling said:

We are tired of war in the industrial field ... Would it not be possible for the employers of this country, on the conclusion of peace, when we have rid ourselves of restrictive legislation to which we have submitted for war purposes, to agree to put their businesses on a new footing by admitting the workmen to some participation, not in profits but in control?

Gosling said that he was not seeking a place for unions to sit on the board of directors or to 'interfere' with matters such as the buying of materials or the selling of products. What the unions wanted was a voice in the daily management of employment – hours, working conditions, pay, and 'the manner and practices of the foreman' – equal with management itself. 'We shall never get any lasting peace except on the lines of democracy,' said Gosling.

The government, too, was anxious to promote close co-operation between the official union leadership and the employers in order to negate the growing power of the shop stewards, particularly as the ending of the war would remove restrictive legislation and allow the stewards to exert more influence on the policies and attitudes of the unions. It was with this object in mind that in 1916 the government set up the Committee on Reconstruction, with a Sub-Committee on Relations between the Employers and the Employed which subsequently became known as the Whitley Committee after its chairman J.H. Whitley, the Speaker of the House of Commons. Amongst the members of the committee were two prominent trade union leaders, J.R. Clynes of the General Workers and Robert Smillie of the Miners.

When the Whitley Committee published its report in 1917 it met with a mixed reception from trade unionists. The more radical elements and the shop stewards saw the whole exercise as an attempt to buttress the capitalist system by making a few cosmetic changes in the hope that they would frustrate efforts to make more fundamental economic and social changes in the direction of socialism. The old style craft unions along with a number of other well-established unions such as the miners opposed the report for different reasons; they saw it as unnecessary interference which would threaten their independence. The TUC leadership was initially indecisive, but eventually gave the report a somewhat less than enthusiastic endorsement. But the general unions and those in the public services like the NUCW saw in the report an opportunity to extend their organisation and influence. In particular they welcomed the Whitley Committee's recommendations for a network of national, district and workplace councils or committees in each industry or service through which union and employer representatives would reach joint decisions on pay and conditions and would resolve grievances between them. The unions felt that such a system would construct a forum which would at least offer the prospect of establishing minimum conditions below which no worker would fall – a not unattractive proposition in the public services where union organisation lagged behind that in the production industries. It was with some optimism, therefore, that unions agreed to participate in Joint Industrial Councils which were set up for the public utilities – such as water, gas and electricity – during 1918. The important development for the Corporation Workers came during the summer of that year when details of a National JIC covering local authority workers in non-trading services were agreed and the union, along with eleven others with members amongst that group of council workers, was allocated two seats on the new body.

The prospects opened up for the NUCW by the establishment of the Joint Industrial Council were matched by a steady consolidation of the union's organisation. Despite the secession of the London Fire Brigade branch in 1918, and an earlier breakaway in 1916 by members employed in the Metropolitan Water Board, membership of the NUCW continued to grow as the losses in London were more than made up by recruitment in other areas. Progress was particularly good in Edinburgh where the union continued to build on the base it had established there in 1909 and it was fast reaching the point where it was becoming the majority union in most of the departments of the city council. Nationally, the membership of the Corporation Workers had reached 12,500 by 1918, an increase of 4,000 during the four years of the war and this prompted the Executive Council to appoint two full-time officers to assist Taylor. In February 1918 Tom McGrath, an Executive member from St.

Women tarring road surfaces during the First World War

Marylebone, was appointed as the union's assistant general secretary and eight months later another Executive member, Joe Burgess from Bermondsey, was appointed as an organiser. Both men had a long association with the union and both were Londoners and thus well known to Taylor, a factor which doubtless influenced their appointment given Taylor's previous unhappy experiences with full-time officers.

Growth in membership was not, however, confined to the NUCW and its rivals among the general unions were steadily increasing both their memberships and their areas of influence; more important, the Municipal Employees' Association – from which the Corporation Workers had split in 1907 – could boast of something like four times the membership of the NUCW and was moving towards a working arrangement with several unions. To meet these developments the executive of the Corporation Workers decided in 1918 to propose a radical change of direction for the union by extending its membership base to cover workers outside of the public services. In other words, in order to meet the competition from the general unions the executive proposed the transformation of the NUCW itself into a general union. The issue was put to the members of the union in a national ballot in which they were asked to register their views on an executive proposal to change the name of the union to the National Union of Corporation and General Workers. The proposition secured the support of 6,266 members with 1,009 voting against; but this response, impressive though it was, failed to meet the requirement that a majority of two-thirds of the total membership – not merely of those voting – was necessary to make such a constitutional change. Having been frustrated in this attempt to recruit beyond the ranks of municipal workers, the Executive Council decided to explore the possibility of establishing a federation of unions with membership bases similar to that of the NUCW. A sub-committee of the EC was set up to examine the situation and to have discussions with interested unions. As a result of this initiative the NUCW organised a conference in December 1919 which was attended by delegates representing the Poor Law Workers' Trade Union, the National Asylum Workers' Union and the Water Works Employees as well as the NUCW itself; the aim was to establish closer working relationships between the unions through some form of federation. But the conference failed to make any progress and the NUCW recognised that it would have to make its own way in what promised to be an extremely turbulent post-war period.

NOTES

1 S & B Webb, op. cit., p.690.
2. See *Municipal Journal*, 6 August, 1915 for the Local Government Board instruction.
3. *The Times*, 9 September 1918.
4. *Holborn and Finsbury Guardian*, 27 September 1918.
5. Holborn Borough Council Minutes, 25 September 1918.
6. Ibid., 23 October 1918.
7. *Pontefract and Castleford Express*, 1 November 1918.
8. *Evening Standard*, 3 September 1918.
9. *The Star*, 7 September 1918.
10. From the file on the dispute in papers of the Industrial Commissioner in the Public Record Office, LAB/2/268/7039/182/1918.
11. The award is published in full in Radford, op. cit., Appendix 2.
12. Note from civil servant to the Industrial Commissioner in papers, op. cit., LAB/2/268/7039/4/1918.
13. See the account of Radford, op. cit., which suggests that 'agreement was reached for the fireman to leave the Corporation works in an orderly manner'. p.73.

12   Whitleyism in a Cold Climate

In April 1919 the new national joint council for local authority workers, formed as a result of the Whitley Committee report, began to function with Taylor and Burgess sitting on the trade union side as representatives of the NUCW. But any expectations that the Whitley Committee report would offer an easy ride to union expansion and a solution of members' grievances were soon dispelled as the new machinery ran into one difficulty after another.

A promising start was made when the employers' representatives agreed to concede the principle of a 47 hour working week, twelve days' annual holiday and the payment of enhanced rates for overtime work. But despite this favourable beginning the two sides were unable to reach any agreement when the important issue of wages appeared on the agenda in the shape of a claim from the trade unions for a national bonus of 30 shillings a week. The resulting deadlock was broken only when the trade union representatives decided to give way because they felt that this was the only way to preserve the existence of the joint council in the first fragile period of its life. The leader of the trade union side – Eldred Hallas MP of the General Workers – explained the unions' decision to act in a conciliatory way when he told the joint council:

> If it were found impossible for the Council to continue its deliberations it would strike a blow at the whole Whitley system, and rather than this should happen we would be prepared to put aside the question of wages and go on to other matters.[1]

It was therefore agreed that wages issues should be left to local authorities and unions to resolve at local level.

While this side-stepping avoided the danger that the joint council would run itself into the ground only a few months after it had been set up it also meant that on the crucial issue of pay the council failed to provide the lead that the unions had been looking for. The compromise by the unions may have secured the continued existence of the council, but it was at a very heavy price.

The failure of the national council to deal with wages was not the only setback for the unions. Very soon another major weakness of the Whitley system was revealed when many local authority employers flatly refused to implement any of the council's decisions with which they disagreed – despite the fact that they were represented on the council and therefore considered to be party to its decisions. When union representatives protested to the employers' side, which they did with almost mathematical regularity, the only solution they were offered by the employers was that the offending local authorities would be reminded that they were 'honourably bound' to implement national joint council decisions. Such reminders made little or no impression and the unions, in an effort to strengthen the authority of the council, decided that agreements made by the council should be legally binding; they made repeated attempts to secure such a commitment from the employers' side and even secured the support of the 1923 annual TUC for the proposition. The employers, doubtless realising that they had established superiority over the union side, refused to budge.

Given the failure of the national council to reach agreement on wages and the refusal of many local authorities to implement national council decisions on other matters, it was not unexpected that the provincial councils, which were set up during 1919 and 1920, showed a similar lack of enthusiasm by the employers' representatives. The provincial councils – with a representation of unions and employers which usually reflected the composition of the national council – consisted of counties grouped together on a geographical basis and charged with the responsibility of establishing joint action on employment matters at local level. Problems of legitimacy arose immediately because many local authorities refused to accept the authority of the new bodies. Some flatly refused to sit on the provincial councils or to have anything at all to do with them. They argued, in a paternalistic fashion which had become characteristic of local councillors who were also employers in private business, that they knew what was best for their workers and they were not going to be dictated to by outsiders. Other local authorities joined the provincial councils at the outset and then withdrew when the councils made decisions which they found unacceptable.[2] Just how widespread these attitudes were was revealed when the national joint council conducted a survey in 1925, five years after provincial councils were first established. The survey showed that less than half of the local authorities were represented on their provincial councils but in some areas – covered by the Western, South Western, Southern and Midland provincial councils – less than a quarter of the local authorities were participating.[3]

Although the employers were much less than enthusiastic to take real action to make the national council and the provincial councils work the unions remained committed to the principles of Whitleyism. They believed that it offered a rational system of collective bargaining and that, despite the initial non-participation of many local authorities, it would eventually lead to the establishment of uniform conditions for similar kinds of work within each provincial council area if not on a national basis. Taylor had no doubts about the value of joint councils, regardless of the difficulties created by reluctant employers. In 1923 he went so far as to say that in two years the joint councils had achieved results which would have taken the unions twenty years to achieve without Whitleyism.[4]

Whatever Taylor's enthusiasm, it is clear that even where the new joint machinery enjoyed the participation of employers it did not present an easy option for the unions because the establishment of the provincial councils coincided with a down-turn in the economy which put pressure on all unions – private and public sector alike – in the wage bargaining process. On the provincial councils covering local authority workers the pressure came through the wage agreements which had a sliding scale built into the bonus payments – which originated to meet wartime inflation – allowing them to fluctuate up and down in line with a cost of living index calculated by the Board of Trade. Until 1920 prices were rising and the index moved upwards, wages were therefore automatically rising under the sliding scale arrangement. But as the depression set in during 1921 prices began to fall and this was reflected in the cost of living index; wage cuts became a regular item on the agenda as provincial councils made quarterly reviews of wages. In an attempt to offset reductions in earnings the NUCW challenged the basis on which the Board of Trade constructed the cost of living index, arguing that it did not reflect price movements in working class household budgets and it should not therefore he used as a basis for pay reductions – regardless of what was said in the pay agreement. Another, and slightly more successful, tactic used by the union was to negotiate the consolidation of all or part of the bonus into the basic minimum wage, thus limiting the proportion of the total pay subject to fluctuation under the sliding scale arrangements. This approach gained some support from Labour-controlled councils, but on the whole provincial councils implemented wage reductions with little effective opposition from the unions. Indeed, on one occasion in 1923 the employers' side of the West Midlands provincial council actually congratulated the trade union side for the way in which it had handled a pay reduction without creating friction.[5]

There was, however, one area in which the NUCW was able to make tangible progress during this difficult period. In the London municipal elections in 1919 the Labour Party swept into control in fourteen borough councils in an historic breakthrough for the new political party of the working class. For the NUCW this breakthrough represented more than a political victory for the party it had helped to construct. It also presented the union with a big opportunity to demonstrate that it could exercise political influence with sympathetic local councillors to win improvements in pay and conditions for its members. Indeed, it may have been this rather than Whitleyism which influenced Taylor's mind when he enthused about the advances made by the union in the early 1920s.

In January 1920 the Fulham borough council organised a wage conference with the objective of securing united action to improve the position of local authority workers in London. The outcome was agreement that councils should aim at a basic minimum rate of 70s 6d a week without a sliding scale attached to it. While some London councils, Woolwich for example, adopted this minimum others set their sights higher. Stepney, Poplar and Bethnal Green all adopted a £4 minimum wage while Battersea opted for 77s. A number of local councils – Woolwich, Stepney and Poplar, for example – incorporated equal pay for men and women doing similar work in the minimum wage standards. So far as London as a whole was concerned the minimum rate set by the London JIC stood at 60s 5d in 1922 and a survey the following year showed that while ten London councils paid below this rate there were many paying above it; it was the latter group which was to come under close government scrutiny through the offices of the District Auditor from 1923 onwards.[6]

In the NUCW stronghold of Bermondsey a minimum wage of £4 and a basic 44 hour working week was established in 1919 when a group of Labour and radical Progressive (Liberal) councillors formed an alliance to push the measure through against the opposition of a Progressive-controlled council. One of the Progressive councillors who defied his party line and voted with the Labour group was NUCW organiser Joe Burgess, who had been elected to the council on a Progressive ticket. Another NUCW member who sat on the Bermondsey council as a Progressive was Isaiah Stokes, secretary of the union's local poor law branch. Unlike Burgess, however, Stokes went along with the Progressive line and voted against the pay increase. Inevitably he came in for heavy criticism from local trade unionists and Labour Party members and although he remained an active members of the NUCW the hostility lasted for a long time. More than a year later the *Bermondsey Labour News* was still attacking Stokes:

> We have a vivid recollection of the occasion when he voted against granting the £4 minimum to Council employees and only a few weeks later went cringing to the Board of Guardians asking that the £4 a week and more should be granted to himself and others engaged in Poor Law Work ... It seems he will fight for the benefits for himself and worry very little about other people.[7]

The 1919 London council elections saw another NUCW member in sharp conflict with the Labour Party – none other than Albin Taylor himself. Taylor had a long and loyal association with the Labour Party and had been a member of

East Ham council for nine years, and secretary of the Labour group on the council from 1911. But, in common with a number of other trade unionists, he found it difficult to respond to the radicalisation of the Labour Party which had taken place during the war years, particularly the emphasis that Labour should stand on its own two feet during elections by opposing the Liberals as well as the Tories because both were equally enemies of the working class. During Taylor's thirty years of public activity he had been accustomed to working in situations where alliances of convenience were frequently made and he was unable to accept the new stance of militant independence adopted by the Labour Party. Consequently, when Labour failed to field a candidate in his constituency during the 1918 general election he had no hesitation in speaking on the Liberal Party platform in support of Sir John Bethall. This infuriated the local Labour Party and early in 1919 it punished Taylor by selecting another candidate to contest his seat at the municipal elections. The Executive Council of the NUCW initially tried to make the best of a difficult situation by saying that while it sympathised with Taylor it would not support him if he decided to stand against the official Labour candidate during the council elections; but it later reversed this decision despite strong protests from the East Ham branch of the union and the local Trades and Labour Council. Taylor decided to go ahead and contest the election against the official Labour candidate, and he defended his presence on the Liberal platform during the general election by saying that he had supported the most advanced candidate and he would have supported the Labour candidate had there been one.[8]

During the election campaign Taylor, describing himself as 'the real Labour candidate' waged a vigorous battle. But this did not prevent the official Labour candidate defeating him by more than 200 votes in a result which the local newspaper described as 'certainly something of a surprise to most people'.[9] For Taylor, now aged 53, this was the last adventure into council elections. He was disillusioned and unable to understand how the Trades and Labour Council could describe him as 'reactionary' after the years of service he had given to the labour movement. What he failed to appreciate was that the politics of the labour movement had matured and in the process had moved further and faster than he was able, or indeed willing, to go.

It was not only in the municipal politics of his own area that Taylor found himself in difficulties. His efforts to strengthen the base of the Corporation Workers in face of growing competition from the general unions also got him into hot water.

The representation of the NUCW on the Whitley Council machinery that had been set up at the end of the war gave a new legitimacy to the union and it began to establish working relations with many of the other unions which had representatives on the trade union sides of the provincial councils. In some areas, however, the old hostility between the Corporation Workers and the general unions persisted, and even increased as Taylor used the opening presented by the Whitley machinery to extend the influence of the union. This was particularly true in Birmingham where, in 1920, the general unions alleged that the NUCW was poaching their members. In response to the allegations, the Corporation Workers issued a recruiting leaflet which displayed all of the characteristics of Taylor's provocative style: 'Poaching is theft, stealing other people's property. In trade unionism the members own the Union not the Union the members, therefore claim your freedom to join the Union of your choice.'

The determination of the Corporation Workers to continue to recruit in Birmingham, despite the attacks by the general workers' unions, was shown in October 1921 when Taylor engaged George Luckman on a one month contract to 'try and organise the Birmingham Corporation workers'.[10] Luckman, a former Birmingham gas worker, had been a branch secretary of the National Union of General Workers but during a period of unemployment he had become involved in a disagreement with that union over funds which he had refused to hand back; he was subsequently expelled from the union and spent four months in prison. After his release from gaol Luckman contacted the NUCW through the Birmingham branch secretary, T.W. Degg, to whom he wrote a letter saying that his ex-workmates at the gas works had asked him to represent them again, and he added, 'they have promised that almost every man will come over to the National Union of Corporation Workers'. Taylor must have seen this letter or been told of its contents by Degg, and been aware of

Luckman's background; but this did not apparently deter him from engaging Luckman.

Once engaged, Luckman made frequent reports to Taylor, giving almost daily accounts of recruiting meetings in gas works, schools, tramway depots and council yards. After a fortnight he informed Taylor: 'Everything points to the fact that the NUGW is losing their [*sic*] members by scores.' The General Workers hit back with a leaflet attacking the Corporation Workers in which it singled out the NUCW's reluctance to take strike action, something which Luckman had apparently been using as a positive virtue in his recruiting campaign. But the General Workers' leaflet put another interpretation on the Corporation Workers' policy. 'Let it be known to your employers that you will not strike, or are not prepared to do so; then goodbye to all progress that you hope to make.' On 19 October the General Workers officially informed Taylor that Luckman had been imprisoned for defaulting the NUGW but, contrary to claims he made later, Taylor did not terminate Luckman's contract at this point. Indeed, he wrote to Luckman saying, 'Your old enemies have written, cannot let you know more, go on and don't bother.' And Luckman did go on, because by the end of the month the membership of the Corporation Workers in Birmingham had increased to the point where new branches were established for gas, electricity and salvage workers.

This incursion into the established territory of the General Workers' Union was seen as a direct challenge by the rivals of the Corporation Workers' on the trade union side of the West Midlands provincial council, and in December 1921 they decided to hit back by refusing to sit alongside the NUCW in any meeting. What this decision really meant was that the representatives of the NUCW were denied access to any provincial council meetings and were thus effectively debarred from any participation in the West Midlands JIC. Taylor made repeated appeals to the national joint council to overrule the West Midlands JIC and reinstate the NUCW representatives, but without success.[11] Taylor also claimed that the Corporation Workers had been excluded from the East Midlands provincial council by the other unions. When a preliminary meeting had been held in October 1919 to set up that provincial council a delegate from the NUCW

Peterborough branch had attended but he had not been
notified of any subsequent meetings. When the provincial
council had been formally constituted and seats allocated to
the various unions the NUCW had not, therefore, been given a
place. This, said Taylor, was deliberate discrimination which
should be remedied; but his main efforts were directed
towards re-establishing the union on the West Midlands
provincial council.

In July 1923 the NUCW decided to refer the matter to the
TUC Disputes Commiteee. It was able to use this process
because in 1920 the TUC – overriding the resolution which
had excluded 'public employee only' unions from affiliation
and the fact that the NUCW was a breakaway organisation –
accepted it into TUC membership (the MEA was permitted
to re-affiliate at the same time). The TUC Disputes
Committee, at a preliminary meeting, called on the trade
union side of the West Midlands JIC to withdraw its embargo
on the Corporation Workers until a proper enquiry had been
conducted.[12] But, with an intransigent attitude which
characterised the situation existing in the West Midlands, the
trade union side refused to meet this request. When a
sub-committee of the Disputes Committee began the enquiry
proper in April 1924, representatives of all the unions involved
attended and put their views. The General Workers' Union
accused the NUCW of trying to recruit in areas where 95 per
cent of the workers were already organised in other unions,
and described this as 'hitting below the belt'. Other unions
were more brutal in their presentation; allegations of bribery
and corruption were made and the MEA said it was
regrettable that other JICs had not followed the example of
the West Midlands and expelled the NUCW.

Putting the NUCW case, Taylor argued that the union had
a right to be represented on provincial councils where its
membership justified it – as in the case of the East and West
Midlands where a quarter of the municipal employees were
members of the NUCW. The activities and, more important,
past activities, of Luckman were raised at the hearing.
Taylor's response was minuted as follows:

With regards to Luckman, the defaulting Secretary, he [Taylor]
knew nothing whatever of this man's career prior to his being

engaged. Luckman was engaged for a month only, and as soon as his history became known to Mr. Taylor he was discharged.[13]

The TUC committee was not, of course, aware of the correspondence that had passed between Taylor and Luckman in October 1921.

After the TUC Disputes Committee had considered the evidence presented to the enquiry it decided that the trade union side had no right to exclude from the provincial council a union which had members amongst the workers covered by that council, and it called for the NUCW to be re-instated. A jubilant Taylor immediately circularised Corporation Workers' branches announcing the victory and proclaiming: 'All branches and members will now be able to hold their heads up and point out that we are a trade union the same as any other and that the Municipal Workers have a right to join if they wish.' But Taylor's jubilation was short lived, because no sooner had the TUC Disputes Committee announced its decision than the General Workers' Union successfully raised the matter directly with the TUC General Council, which ruled that the TUC had no power to decide on the eligibility or otherwise of unions to become members of Joint Industrial Councils. This decision brushed aside the Corporation Workers' claim for representation on the East and West Midlands JICs and many years were to pass before it was finally to establish its position on those councils.

The clash between the NUCW and the general unions in the West Midlands was symptomatic of the conflicts that had developed between many unions as they sought to preserve themselves from erosion by the economic recession of the early 1920s. By the end of the 1921 the number out of work had passed the 2,000,000 mark and the effects of this, plus the defensive stance unions were forced to adopt to resist the downward pressure on wages, weakened workers' commitment to trade unionism and squeezed the membership of unions. The biggest impact of the recession was felt by unions in the private sector, some of which suffered considerable membership losses. But unions in the public sector, while not experiencing anything like the losses of unions in the private sector, did not escape unscathed, as the NUCW discovered as its membership slid down by some 3,000 after reaching an all time high of 16,500 in 1920. Faced with declining memberships, unions increased their recruiting activities to compensate for losses; conflict developed as rival unions competed for new members with less regard for spheres of influence and established areas of membership interest than had been observed between unions in earlier – and easier – times. Unions operating exclusively in the public services, like the NUCW, came under particular pressure as unions which operated across the board, like the general unions, sought to expand their membership in the more stable public sector to compensate for losses in the private sector.

While they were engaged in inter-union struggles for members the unions were also suffering from another effect of the economic recession. Their finances were pinched between falling contribution income on the one hand and the need to spend more money on recruitment and organisation campaigns on the other; as a result many union balance sheets began to take on a very unhealthy look.

The overall effect of this situation prompted many unions to look towards amalgamation as an answer to their difficulties. Early in 1921 the Executive of the NUCW made an attempt to reach an agreement with the General Workers' Union and the MEA on the formation of some form of federation. But, not surprisingly, given the uneasy relations between the Corporation Workers and those unions, discussions did not get beyond preliminary stages before collapsing. Around the same time the NUCW also approached the Firemen's Trade Union and the National Asylum Workers' Union, but these approaches also came to nothing. Undaunted by these failures the 1922 NUCW national conference instructed the EC to conduct a national ballot of members on whether they were 'in favour of Amalgamation with Unions catering solely for Corporation Workers'. If the intention was to reinforce the policy of making organisational link-ups with other unions, it failed; the ballot returned 1,704 members voting in favour and 3,742 against. At the 1923 national conference the president, D. Stephen, commented: 'Whilst I fully believe amalgamation must eventually come, I am sorry to say the majority of our members are not ready for it.'

Other unions were more successful. In 1922 the Transport

National Union of Corporation Workers

Reg. No. 1386 T. Offices: 138 First Avenue, London, E 12.

DUNDEE BRANCH

TO CONSIDER:—

(1) *Union by Industry, by Craft, or General.*

(2) *Provisions of the Local Government and other Officers Superannuation Act, 1922.*

(3) *Whitley Councils for Public Services.*

A MASS MEETING of DUNDEE CORPORATION WORKERS

WILL TAKE PLACE ON

FRIDAY FIRST, 24th Nov., at 7 p.m.

AT THE

Ex=Service Men's Club, Nethergate.

Secretary, D. SPENCE,
42 Court Street, Clepington.

CONTRIBUTIONS—Men—Entrance Fee, 1/-, then 4d per Week.
 Do. Women— „   6d, then 2d „

BENEFITS—At Death, for Member up to £10; for his Wife up to £5.
 £50 to £100 Permanent Accident Disablement. 1/8 per
 day Accident Benefit. Grants for Elections. With
 Efforts to Improve Conditions of Employment.

An Industrial Union for Corporation Workers only
——— Assets, £29,000. ———

Come and Learn.   *Unity is Strength*

DURHAM & SON, LTD., DUNDEE.

Handbill issued in the early 1920s
by the Dundee branch of the NUCW

and General Workers' Union was formed; centred on unions representing the dockers and transport workers it was able to claim an impressive membership of 300,000. Two years later, in 1924, the union which had parted company with Taylor fourteen years earlier – the Municipal Employees' Association – ceased to exist when it amalgamated with National Union of General Workers and other unions to form the 350,000 strong National Union of General and Municipal Workers. This emergence of the general unions as large and expanding power bases was to have important consequences for the whole of the trade union movement. Taylor, drawing on past experience, was quick to recognise this. In a speech to the 1924 TUC he urged the General Council to ensure that fair play and justice be given to all when disputes arose between unions: 'I am very suspicious in this matter and I sincerely hope that it will not be possible for large bodies of persons to have their way because of their numbers,' said Taylor in a direct and obvious reference to the general unions.[14]

NOTES

1. National Joint Council (Non Trading Services) Minutes, 9 May, 28 May, 30 July 1919.
2. See the case of Kent County Council's refusal to sit on the Council for Kent, Surrey, East and West Sussex. Southern and Home Counties Provincial Council Minutes, 20 July, 1920. For an example of a council withdrawing, see the case of Reading in NJC minutes, 4 March, 6 May 1920.
3. NJC Minutes, 3 July 1925.
4. *Wood Green Sentinel*, 23 September 1923.
5. West Midlands JIC Minutes, 25 April 1923.
6. PRO LAB 2/1361/185/879/123.
7. *Bermondsey Labour News*, No. 11, February 1921.
8. *East Ham Echo*, 17 October 1919.
9. Ibid., 7 November 1919.
10. This and subsequent quotations are taken from a file of correspondence and papers relating to the West Midlands episode.
11. Minutes of National JIC Minutes, 3 March; 5 May; 6 October 1922.
12. TUC Disputes Committee Minutes, 26 October 1923.
13. Ibid., 17 April 1924.
14. Annual report of TUC, 1924.

13 A Pioneer Departs

Clashes with the general unions and competition for members were not the only problems to confront the NUCW during the turbulent years of the early 1920s. Internally the union faced organisational difficulties as it sought to adapt itself to a new situation and to establish its role within a changing trade union movement. Often these difficulties manifested themselves as differences between a leadership concerned to consolidate and a rank and file impatient to advance. In such a situation it was inevitable that the general secretary should find himself at the centre of the arguments, and given Albin Taylor's forceful character it was equally inevitable that the arguments would frequently become highly personalised.

At the centre of the union the EC itself was adapting to recently introduced changes which had altered the character of the Executive and the relationships between the EC and the general secretary. The 1919 national conference made a radical change to the rule relating to the election of the EC when the distribution of Executive seats on a district basis – which had given London members a favourable position on the Executive – was scrapped. As a consequence the EC elected in 1920 contained seven members – half of the total – who came from outside London and who occupied seats they had won in open, nation-wide contest. The 1919 conference made another important change in the rules by depriving Taylor of his vote on the EC, thereby emphasising his role as a paid servant of the union. These two changes created a new alignment of forces at the centre of the union.

This new EC was soon confronted with a major problem when the union's assistant general secretary, Tom McGrath, died in January 1921 after a period of ill health. Taylor refused to sanction the appointment of a successor on the grounds that there was insufficient work to warrant the employment of an assistant general secretary. His attitude provoked complaints from a number of branches and the Bermondsey clerical branch in particular began a campaign for a resolution to be put before the EC on the appointment of a new assistant general secretary. Taylor's response was immediate and characteristic; he issued a series of circulars to branches in which he condemned the action of the Bermondsey clerical branch and its Executive Council member, W. Loveland. Taylor argued that with the introduction of the Whitley Council machinery much of the work previously performed by full-time officers had become unnecessary, and he supported this argument by telling members: 'The last eighteen months have been the easiest of my life.' Financial considerations also appeared to weigh heavily on Taylor's mind, for he pointed to the fact that the cost of wages and expenses for full-time officers took half of the union's income.

From these general points, Taylor became more specific – and personal. The full-time organiser for the London area, Joe Burgess, came in for special criticism, particularly for his failure to recruit new members and thus help the union's finances. Wrote Taylor: 'I quite believe he does his best but where is the result, for that we are paying £8/10 a week or £422 per annum.' Even the not long dead McGrath did not escape Taylor's wrath. McGrath was accused of doing what he wanted to do and not what the organisation required and, said Taylor, McGrath was responsible for generating 'contention' in the union.

The circulars to branches also showed that Taylor was extremely suspicious of the motives of those who were advocating that a new assistant general secretary should be appointed. 'There must be some object behind it ... Position must be wanted for self or friend or a desire to get at me,' Taylor told the branches. And he followed this with a wide ranging swipe at members of the EC. 'It may be "I am on the Executive Council I will rule and sway, my will shall be done, and if a mere official gets in my way, we'll gag, bind or cut him".' Finally, in what was obviously a warning to his opponents, Taylor recalled the memories of the dispute that had split the Municipal Employees' Association asunder fourteen years before.

This controversy may lead to another MEA dispute, if it does it will again be over officials, official positions and money ... It is such a doubtful blessing I am determined to have no more of it while I am General Secretary.

In an effort to settle the argument, a special meeting of the Executive Council was called in October 1921; but tempers were running so high that even the calling of the meeting itself became the subject of argument. Taylor declared that such a meeting was against the rules of the union and before business could begin it was necessary for the president to give a ruling that – contrary to Taylor's view – the EC did have a right to consider the matter. A long discussion at the meeting failed to reach a conclusion on whether an assistant general secretary should be appointed and finally the Executive elected a committee to look into the dispute. The committee met only once, when it received a report from Taylor outlining the work which he and the clerk performed and which, Taylor believed, demonstrated that an assistant general secretary was not necessary. Like the full Executive Council, the committee could not reach any satisfactory conclusion and the matter was once again shunted elsewhere, this time to the annual conference. At the conference, in July 1922, the Bermondsey clerical branch made certain the matter was discussed by tabling a resolution which called for the appointment of a successor to Tom McGrath. But after a lengthy debate the resolution was defeated by 137 to 119 on a card vote; the issue was settled and Taylor's view had prevailed, but the acrimony the whole affair had generated was something which the union could have done without.

The dispute over the appointment of an assistant general secretary was not the only internal difficulty confronting the EC; no sooner had it been resolved than another dispute, this time involving the members in Scotland, had come to a head. By 1921 the Edinburgh branch had grown to 1,600 members, making it the strongest in the union. The members ranged across all of the council's departments and included gas and electricity workers whom the union represented on the Scottish JIC for those industries. Although the branch secretary, James Stewart, provided an able service in the locality, it was natural that, as the branch grew in size and diversity, a demand should arise from the members for the appointment of a full-time organiser. Taylor resisted this demand and argued that there was no evidence to suggest that a full-time officer could win any better improvements in pay and conditions than could be secured by voluntary officials. Appealing to the Edinburgh members to put their energies in more constructive directions, Taylor reiterated his belief in action through the ballot box when he told them, 'You will not beat the City [*sic*] Council by one or even two paid officials; thirty to forty good Labour men on the Council may.' But the Edinburgh members were not diverted by such a prospect and despite Taylor's personal opposition they continued to press their demand for a full-time official. By January 1924 they had built up sufficient support on the EC to win a vote for the appointment of a full-time district secretary by seven votes to five. Four months later Michael Carabine, an Edinburgh lamplighter, was appointed to the post and his first task was to draw up a major wage claim.

With the wages of NUCW members in Edinburgh lagging behind those of workers in surrounding towns, Carabine was assured of enthusiastic support for the wage claim from a branch which had been flexing its muscles for some time. The strength of feeling was demonstrated when in September the Edinburgh members voted by a majority of nearly four to one to take strike action if the council did not improve wages. This determination by the NUCW members was equally matched by a firm response from the council, which promptly rejected the claim for a 54 shilling minimum wage when it was lodged by the union.[1] Lengthy negotiations followed during which Taylor made frequent visits to Edinburgh, apparently to restrain the members – who by this time had reached fever pitch – from staging an immediate walk out. But by the beginning of December it had become obvious that all of the talking had produced nothing from the council and the members were not prepared to hold back any longer. Carabine therefore gave the council formal notice that strike action would start on December 12; the union then waited to see what kind of response this ultimate threat would provoke from the council.[2] The response came almost immediately. The council warned that all men who failed to report for work would be instantly dismissed, and it added the more sinister warning that it would take legal action – which could lead to imprisonment – against the workers in the water, electricity and gas departments, who were constrained from taking industrial action under the 1875 Conspiracy and Protection of Property Act. The severity of these threatened reprisals shocked Taylor, Carabine and the Edinburgh branch leadership; the strike notice was withdrawn and negotiations re-opened with the council firmly established in the dominant position.[3] The council repeated an offer made several months earlier in the knowledge that this time the union would recommend its members to accept it. A minimum wage of 53 shillings was offered to workers in the council's non-trading departments – which accounted for a little over a quarter of the workforce – and the claim for the remainder was sent to an arbitration hearing which, in June 1925, rejected most of the union's demands, including a claim by firemen for the restoration of a 5 per cent pay cut. The only real gain made by the union during the dispute was a further increase in the size of the Edinburgh branch, which also established a white collar section as a result of an influx of staff from the council's offices.

While it was dealing with the situation in Edinburgh the EC suddenly found another problem on its plate when, in July 1924, Taylor unexpectedly asked the Executive to consider his retirement. He gave age, ill health and dissatisfaction as the reasons prompting his desire to retire. There can be no doubt that this decision by Taylor came as a complete surprise to the EC because only twelve months before it had informed members that the general secretary had no plans for early retirement. The 1922 national conference had passed a resolution instructing the EC to make financial arrangements to ensure that Taylor received a pension when he retired. But the Executive took no action on the resolution and in a statement to the 1923 conference it explained that it had given careful consideration to the matter and remarked, 'that the General Secretary has not asked to be released; shows but little sign of old age or inability; there is no complaint as to delay or inconvenience.' For these reasons, said the EC, it regarded the resolution as premature and recommended that it be 'discharged', a recommendation which was endorsed by the conference delegates.

The EC statement was undoubtedly inspired by the views

Jim Bradley, the park keeper who became spokesman for the
London firemen during their dispute with the LCC

which had been expressed by Taylor himself when the 1922 resolution was discussed by the Executive and doubtless, as in the normal course of events, he had himself drafted the statement. Yet a year after members had been categorically assured of the general secretary's continuing service, Taylor had suddenly changed his mind, and giving ill health, age and dissatisfaction as his reasons for wanting retirement, he negated every point that had been made in the EC's statement to the 1922 conference. As if to compensate for this sudden change of attitude, Taylor agreed to continue in office until October 1925; he thus gave the EC more than twelve months in which to find and install his successor. It was not until the summer of 1925, when it set up a special committee with powers to make an appointment, that the EC gave any serious consideration to the matter. Advertisements were placed in the labour press and attracted no fewer than 180 applications for the post. These were scrutinised by the special committee and eleven applicants were selected for interview. On 11 August 1925, London building worker Jack Wills emerged from the interview as the successor to Albin Taylor.

Precisely what particular circumstances prompted Taylor to tell the EC that he wanted to quit as general secretary must remain a matter of conjecture. But whatever the final event which determined Taylor's action, a review of the accumulated historical evidence indicates that his decision was the logical outcome of the convergence of a variety of factors – all of which played a part in the making of that decision.

Despite his long and active role in the labour movement Taylor was not basically a political animal. Although he had been a member of the Social Democratic Federation in the late 1880s when he began his trade union activities, there is no evidence to suggest that Taylor had absorbed in a permanent sense any of the Marxist ideology which inspired the SDF. Indeed, his extensive work within the labour movement appears to have been carried out without any deep sense of *ideological* motivation; his sole aim was to win a better deal for the workers. To Taylor, politics were primarily a pragmatic approach to the immediate problems facing the workers in general and the members of his union in particular; he did not see politics as the expression of a fundamental class conflict in which the workers were struggling to establish themselves as the dominant class in society. In this he was no different from many other union leaders of his generation, as evidenced by those who were elected as Liberal MPs and local councillors even after a strong socialist tendency had emerged in the unions to demand independent working class action. Taylor's action in supporting a Liberal candidate in the 1918 election, and his inability to understand why this should have caused personal attacks to be made upon him by men in the labour movement whom he regarded as colleagues, demonstrate a degree of political naivety. He failed to grasp the fact that the time had passed when 'labour' in political terms was a convenient label which could loosely be attached to almost any candidate who promised friendly assistance to union leaders when elected. As the voice of radical socialism became louder and stronger, Taylor, like many other trade union leaders who were 'labour' in what can be called the old fashioned sense of the word, found himself increasingly estranged from the mainstream in the labour movement.

But politics, in the limited sense that he accepted them, were very important to Taylor in that they were central to his approach to trade unionism. Throughout his long years of trade union activity Taylor made no secret of the fact that he was opposed to the use of industrial action to gain concessions from the employers. Indeed, he made the lack of strike action by the NUCW – and the other unions which he had led – a major feature in his recruitment and organising campaigns. In speeches, leaflets and reports he constantly emphasised the gains that the union had won without resorting to strikes which, he argued, caused the workers to lose more than they gained. In place of industrial action Taylor advocated political action through the ballot box to elect local councillors who were sympathetic to the union and were prepared to support its claims for better wages and conditions. For Taylor this was perhaps the ultimate in politics: the ability of municipal workers to elect employers who were prepared to give them a fair deal. He was also prepared to argue, as he did with the Edinburgh members, that Labour councillors were an effective substitute for full-time organisers.

Taylor's emphasis on local politics as a major trade union tactic in collective bargaining coupled with his reluctance to become involved in strike action produced some successes; but they were limited in application and fragile in durability. Economic factors and the more determined attitudes adopted by unions as they grew in size, experience and confidence placed the tactics advocated by Taylor under increasing pressure and this made his style of leadership appear somewhat conservative alongside the more radical attitudes which became prevalent after the 1914-18 war.

Coincidental with the radicalisation of political and trade union attitudes was a major development in trade union organisation. Two large and powerful general unions emerged from amalgamations – the TGWU and the GMWU, whose influence impinged sharply on the Corporation Workers' area of activity in local government. Throughout his trade union life Taylor had been caught up in the inter-union competition and conflict which was a characteristic of this period of development in trade union history. But by the early 1920s a situation had arisen where the NUCW was in grave danger of being overwhelmed by events. The alliance of unions to squeeze the NUCW from membership of the provincial councils in the East and West Midlands and the refusal of the TUC General Council to take action to safeguard the Corporation Workers' position were clear indicators of how sharp the competition – and conflict – had become between the NUCW and the general unions, which were growing in strength and influence inside the trade union movement.

When the MEA ceased to exist as a result of the merger which created the GMWU, part of Taylor would doubtless have felt a sense of satisfaction in seeing the demise of an organisation which, since the 1907 split, he had seen as a personal as well as a trade union rival. But on the other hand Taylor was astute enough to recognise that although the MEA had ceased to exist as a separate entity, its organisational base and its potential for expansion at the expense of the NUCW had been strengthened by its absorption into a general union. The prospect before the NUCW, therefore, was continuing and increasing problems with the general unions and it is perhaps not without significance that Taylor announced his wish to retire in 1924, the year in which the GMWU was formed. If this did influence Taylor's decision it is understandable. He was 58 years old, and after 35 years of hard and dedicated work in the trade union movement he was general secretary of what was, in comparison with the newly emerged general unions, a very small fish which would need to work hard if it was to avoid being gulped down by one of its bigger brethren. If Taylor thought that he had suffered enough aggravation through inter-union conflict over the years, and that it would be better if someone else took over the leadership of the NUCW in the stormy period that loomed ahead, there can be few who could have honestly disagreed with him.

There is also some indication that, despite his assertion to the contrary when resisting the appointment of a successor to McGrath, Taylor found that the burden of administrative work at the union's head office had become more than he could cope with – particularly as his experience had equipped him better to deal with organisational work in the field than with administrative routine at head office. And the fact that nearly half of the unions's branches were in the provinces while only one full-time organiser – Carabine in Scotland – was based outside London meant that the amount of branch business carried out by correspondence from head office would have been considerable. The difficulties this created were indicated by the president, W. Loveland, in his address to the 1926 national conference when he outlined some of the changes that had been made at the union's head office since Taylor had retired. In addition to purchasing new equipment and employing an additional clerk the president reported that 'new systems of office routine' had been introduced:

> One of which was to promptly forward copies of complete correspondence dealt with to the Branches concerned so that they [the branches] were fully and quickly acquainted of the progress of all matters in which they were interested.

The president also gave details of a new method of dealing with the union's financial business, which as it involved payments from all the branches, imposed quite a work load on head office. The president concluded with the comment, 'I think we can now safely say that our Office had been put in order, and placed on a business footing.' Even when allowances had been made for the proverbial new broom sweeping clean, it is apparent from the president's remarks that the EC was aware of shortcomings that had existed at the union's head office – particularly in dealing with provincial branches which relied on the office to act on their behalf in the absence of a full-time organiser in their areas.

All of these problems obviously imposed a considerable burden on Taylor and his ability to cope with them was not helped by the increasingly autocratic style he adopted and which cannot but have soured relations between him and the EC, which was less inclined to accept the general secretary's lead without question than it had been in earlier years. Taylor had always been something of a stormy petrel but he attracted considerable personal loyalty, especially from those who had known him in the MEA, taken his side in the struggles and split of 1907 and then joined him in the NUCW to build a new union from scratch. But even when this is taken into account, the attacks on Executive members by Taylor in circulars to branches – during the dispute about the appointment of an assistant general secretary, for example – would have put serious strains even on old loyalties. At the point when Taylor most needed the support and encouragement of the EC, therefore, his idiosyncratic style of leadership caused him to antagonise those who could best have assisted him – and the union – to cope with a difficult set of circumstances.

Nothing, however, can detract from the pioneering role that Taylor played in laying the foundation stones of the union. And, despite his aberration in 1918, it cannot be denied that his promotion of labour representation – particularly on local authorities – made an important contribution to the development of the Labour Party. Any objective examination of history must accept that Taylor, perhaps because of his personal style of leadership, displayed a tenacity of purpose which made it possible for municipal workers – who were badly paid for doing unpleasant jobs in wretched conditions – to achieve a new sense of dignity. And it was a dignity which expressed itself in the existence of their union, which Taylor led until his retirement in 1925.

NOTES

1. Edinburgh Town Council Minutes, 9 October 1924.
2. *Edinburgh Evening News*, 5 December 1924.
3. Ibid., 11 December 1924.

14 NUPE is Born

When Jack Wills became the general secretary of the Corporation Workers in October 1925 he was already a well-established figure in the labour movement. Born in the London Borough of Poplar in June 1877, he served an apprenticeship as a bricklayer and became an active member of the Operative Bricklayer's Society while still a young man. When the ideas of industrial unionism and syndicalism began to influence the militant sections of the trade union movement in the period prior to the 1914-18 war, Wills, whose attitudes were firmly on the left wing, rapidly aligned himself with the new movement. He became an active propagandist for the Industrial Syndicalist Education League which argued that industrial unions were the organisations which, by using the weapon of the general strike, could bring about social change and create a socialist society. He featured prominently in the debates on syndicalism and industrial unionism which took place at the TUC and was particularly active in the Amalgamation Committee, an organisation which campaigned for the amalgamation of unions on industrial lines. His belief in industrial unionism was strengthened after the London building workers were defeated in a major strike in 1914, during which Wills had travelled the country to win the support of workers outside London. From the experience of this strike Wills and other prominent rank and file leaders of the building workers decided to establish a single union for all building and construction workers, skilled or unskilled. The new organisation, the Building Workers' Industrial Union, was launched in August 1914 – with strong opposition from the conservative leaders of the traditional craft unions – and Wills was elected its general secretary.[1]

Wills's interest in politics began when, while still a young apprentice, he was attracted by the Marxist ideas of Hyndman, and joined the Social Democratic Federation

Jack Wills, union general secretary, 1925-1933, with his family

which Hyndman led. With the growth of the Labour Party Wills became active in the local politics of the South East London borough of Bermondsey where he lived; he became an alderman on the borough council there in 1909 and eventually mayor. He also won a seat on the local board of guardians and became leader of the Labour group. These activities in local politics brought him into close contact with the NUCW which had a number of strong and active branches in the Bermondsey area and he rapidly established a reputation as a champion of the council workers. In 1921, for example, he led the opposition to a proposal by the leader of the Bermondsey Labour group, Dr Alfred Salter, that the minimum wage of Bermondsey council workers should be reduced to the basic London JIC level.[2]

With such a pedigree in the trade union and labour movement, Wills was well equipped to take on rival candidates when he was interviewed by the special committee which appointed the new NUCW general secretary. But some of the other candidates were also able to present impressive records of activity in the labour movement. They included a former president of the Corporation Workers, D.G. Stephens from Edinburgh; the former NUCW organiser Henry Bye; the secretary of the Cumberland Colliery Engineers, John Allen; and two men who had played a leading role in the labour and trade union movement and whose outstanding abilities were subsequently to secure them Cabinet appointments in the 1945 Labour government – Chuter Ede and Manny Shinwell. Despite such strong competition Wills was established as the favourite in an eliminating ballot and at the final stage he beat Chuter Ede by eighteen votes to four.

One of the first decisions of the Executive Council after Wills had taken office was to accept a recommendation from him that the union's head office should be moved from the back room it occupied in a private house in Manor Park to Bermondsey, where two offices were available in the local Labour Party building at a reasonable rent of £1 a week. For Wills the move had distinct advantages; he had only a ten minute walk from his home to the office which was also close on hand for him to perform his duties as a member of the Bermondsey council and the local board of guardians.

At this time the union was very influential in the local politics of Bermondsey; NUCW organiser Joe Burgess and the Bermondsey Poor Law branch secretary Isaiah Stokes – both of whom had parted company with the Liberals – sat alongside Wills on the Labour group which dominated the Bermondsey council. The union had used its influence on the council to help improve the wages and conditions of the borough employees and to increase the scales of relief paid to the local unemployed. Soon after Wills was appointed NUCW general secretary the close relationship between the union and the council came under strong attack from Labour's opponents, who alleged that councillors and guardians with vested interests were squandering public money. Stokes was singled out for particular attack and demands were made that he should resign his seat on the council because there was a conflict of interest between his responsibilities as a councillor, his job as a relieving officer for the board of guardians and his union post as a local NUCW branch secretary.[3]

In many other boroughs all over London, Labour-controlled councils were coming under attack from a variety of right-wing elements who objected to the radical policies being implemented by the councils. The first major confrontation with the government had taken place in 1921-22 when the Labour council at Poplar refused to levy a rate on behalf of London-wide public authorities, such as the London County Council, until a more equitable system of financing unemployment relief was introduced. At the time the poorer boroughs, such as Poplar, had to raise large sums of money through the rates to pay local unemployment relief while the wealthier boroughs with lower levels of unemployment were able to levy lower rates. By refusing to raise a rate for the other public authorities the Poplar councillors, led by George Lansbury, were making a dramatic protest against this unfair system and publicising their proposals for an alternative system of pooled rates under which the wealthy boroughs would subsidise the poorer ones. The Poplar councillors ended up in court and thirty of them were sent to prison where they remained for six weeks. But the protest was effective because public support grew to the point where it caused the government to back down and concede the principle of a pooled common fund for poor law relief.[4]

This successful defiance by the Poplar councillors caused their opponents to seek other areas of attack, and the £4 minimum wage paid to Poplar council workers became the target as the Municipal Alliance (Labour's opponents on the council), ratepayers' associations and local employers voiced objections to Poplar council paying wages higher than those established by the London JIC. This campaign received a boost in May 1923 when the District Auditor – a public official with responsibility for checking local authority accounts – declared that Poplar was overpaying its workers and threatened to surcharge the councillors for the amount he alleged they had overpaid. Poplar council claimed that it had the right as an employer to pay its workers whatever wages it thought fit, and it sought to establish that right by taking the matter to the courts. But when the case finally reached the House of Lords in April 1925 the Law Lords upheld the District Auditor's decision by declaring that £4 was an unreasonable payment and it should be reduced to bring it into line with the wages of London municipal workers paid according to JIC rates.

Following this victory the District Auditor turned his attention to other London boroughs where workers employed by Labour-controlled councils enjoyed wages and conditions above JIC levels. Bethnal Green, Woolwich, Battersea, Stepney and Bermondsey were all instructed to cut wages. This action by a non-elected public official, as Labour councillors called the District Auditor, met with considerable opposition in the labour movement; not least by the councillors themselves who, in the words of the *Municipal Journal*, objected to being 'summoned by a public official, acting as both prosecutor and judge'.[5] The NUCW, recognising that the situation posed a serious threat to its policies of using influence with Labour councils to improve pay and conditions, sprang to the defence of the councils under attack and in 1926 Wills raised the issue to a national level when he successfully proposed a resolution at the TUC which called on the trade union movement to protest against the surcharging policies of the District Auditor.[6]

In February 1927 Wills was a member of a TUC deputation to the Minister of Health, Neville Chamberlain, who had government responsibility for the matter, to put the case against surcharging. But Chamberlain was neither interested in nor impressed by the arguments put by Wills and the other TUC representatives and said that he was powerless to interfere with the District Auditor. In reality the government had already made up its mind further to strengthen the position of the District Auditor by introducing a new law which would not only give him power to disallow 'unreasonable' wages, as defined by the Poplar decision, and to surcharge councillors for the excess but would also disqualify such councillors from holding public office for five years. Wills saw this as a clear example of class legislation, and he told members in the July 1927 issue of the NUCW Journal:

> The Tories, finding that they have lost all power and influence on a considerable number of Town Councils and Boards of Guardians, have set themselves to thwart these bodies which have come under Labour dominance ... Strangle the Councils, say the Tories at Westminster, tie them up with Whitehall Red Tape until they are helpless and harmless, harass them with legal action.

The new legislation, the Audit (Local Authorities) Bill, generated considerable opposition right across the spectrum – from unions who saw it as an attack on the wages of council workers to progressive-minded individuals who saw the Bill as an abuse of central government power over local democracy. The *Municipal Journal* summed up the situation in December 1927 when it commented:

> Probably no Bill in recent years has been placed on the statute book with more misgivings ... Common sense assures the British citizen that local government will not become a predatory practice merely because two or three borough councils paid more than the current rate of wages to their lavatory attendants.[7]

But despite the widespread opposition the new legislation was pushed through parliament and councillors found themselves faced with the grim prospect of being both surcharged and disqualified from office if they did not submit to the District Auditor and reduce the wages of their workers. The left wing of the London labour movement – which at this time still included some Communists as individual members of the Labour Party – attempted to mobilise resistance to the new law. The Stepney council argued:

> Since there will always be sufficient representatives to take the place of those disqualified ... no legislation of this nature forced upon the electorate will produce its intended effect of modifying the progressive and enlightened administration of duly elected authorities.[8]

In Bethnal Green the Communist mayor led a fight against the new law and told the electorate:

> There is no question on our part of obeying the law and acting in a legal manner, our object is to defeat what lies behind the application of the law. We shall always be prepared to break the capitalist law in the interests of the workers. Our opponents use the law in order to cripple the workers and reduce their standards of life.[9]

But those who were prepared to defy the new law were in a minority in the London Labour Party; the majority accepted the view of the Bermondsey Labour leader Dr Salter when he said that defeat was inevitable and further resistance was impossible and useless. Workers, he said, would have to learn the lesson and organise for the next election when 'these and other things can be put right'.[10] The labour movement was forced on to the defensive and one by one the offending councils fell into line and, in consultation with their workers, reduced wages.

The assault by the District Auditor was not the only attack on wages to confront the NUCW. Encouraged by so-called economy campaigns which the government used to promote expenditure cuts by public authorities, a few local councils in London were tempted to try to make some quick savings by falling back on the old device of employing private contractors. Edmonton called in the private contractors in 1923 as did Wandsworth, when it turned over its refuse disposal to a large scale operator who had been working in the nearby borough of Lambeth for three years; Finsbury turned its refuse service over to contractors in 1925.[11] The objective of all these councils was to save money on wages by using private contractors who were not obliged to meet even the minimum JIC standards on pay and conditions. As one Edmonton councillor commented, in words reminiscent of the 1890s, 'No matter how low the contractors' price might be, he was going to make the contract pay, either by underpaying the dustmen or neglecting work.' This prediction was confirmed by experience and the Edmonton council was forced to revert to direct labour after the contractor had proved incapable of providing a satisfactory service.[12] In Finsbury, too, the rate of collecting fell by almost half in the first week of the contract.[13] Municipal engineers, who were responsible for organising many of the services provided by local authorities, had a general dislike of private contracting; as one of them made clear in April 1925:

> There is not much that can be said in favour of contract labour with regard to refuse collection and street scavenging. Past experience has proved that where tact, cleanliness and unfailing regularity are required, the employment of contract labour will mean that the authority will be inundated with complaints.[14]

This was a view shared by most local authorities in the country, who accepted that for refuse collection, street cleansing and other public health services private contracting was a thing of the past. Thus, despite the efforts of a few borough councils in London, the NUCW was able to limit the use of contractors as a wage-cutting weapon.

The attack on the wages and conditions of local council workers was paralleled by a similar but much more fundamental assault on workers in private industry, as employers attempted to cut wage costs to meet the economic crisis which was hitting their profit margins. Nowhere was this more true than in the coal mining industry, which was setting the scene for a major confrontation between labour and capital.

Ownership of the coal mining industry was highly fragmented between some 1,400 colliery companies with an additional burden of thousands of landowners who had the right to payment on every ton of coal raised. Lack of capital investment over many years meant that the industry lagged behind in mechanised coal production which, in turn, meant that labour accounted for a high proportion of total costs. Completely ill-equipped to withstand the economic crisis of the 1920s, the coal mining industry was dealt a further blow when the government decided to return to the Gold Standard in April 1925 and coal exporters were faced with the need to reduce prices in order to maintain their markets overseas. Inevitably the coalowners sought to solve their problems at the expense of the miners, and in June 1925 they gave one month's notice of their intention to terminate the existing agreement with the miners. They then attempted to force on the miners a package which would cut wages and introduce a new formula for pay determination which would guarantee a certain level of profit but eliminate the guaranteed minimum standard wage. The trade union movement, recognising that a defeat for the miners would be a prelude to a wider attack on the wages of all workers, made preparations to come to the defence of the miners. A special conference of union executives called by the TUC General Council met on 30 July 1925, and backed plans for an embargo on the movement of coal if the miners were locked out and empowered the General Council to give financial support to the miners. Unprepared at this stage to face a battle with the unions the government, just a day after the meeting of union executives, announced that it would subsidise the coal mining industry for nine months and that meanwhile a Royal Commission would examine the problems of the industry.

The unions saw this as a victory, but in reality the government was buying time to prepare for a show-down with the miners and, if necessary, with the whole trade union movement. The hard-line Home Secretary, Sir William Joynson-Hicks, put the situation clearly in perspective when he warned that the danger was not over: 'Sooner or later this thing has got to be fought out. Is England [*sic*] to be governed by Parliament and the Cabinet, or by a handful of trade union leaders?' And in preparation for the fight Joynson-Hicks drew up a memorandum for the Cabinet which set out in minute detail the steps which the government should take to meet the threat of a widespread strike. While the government was putting this plan into effect a well-orchestrated propaganda campaign was mounted to maximise opposition to the unions; this included the setting up of bodies such as the Organisation for the Maintenance of Supplies to provide volunteers – mainly from the middle class – for strike breaking activities. Ostensibly the OMS was a private voluntary organisation, but Joynson-Hicks gave it an official seal of approval when he told parliament that anyone who registered with the OMS was carrying out a patriotic duty.

As the months slid by negotiations involving the coalowners, the Miners' Federation, the government and the TUC failed to reach any agreements. Then on Friday 30 April 1926, the coalowners acted and locked out a million miners in an attempt to force them to accept the new terms of employment. Up to this point trade union leaders were still hoping that an agreement could be reached. A conference of union executives had been convened by the TUC General Council to receive a report of negotiations that were taking place, and when this met for its first session on Thursday 29 April, it endorsed the efforts of the General Council to secure 'an honourable settlement' and agreed that negotiations should continue so long as the miners were not locked out. When the conference reconvened on 1 May the miners had been locked out despite the fact that talks were still going on between the TUC and the government; the conference responded to this new situation by endorsing plans for a phased nation-wide stoppage of work commencing on the morning of 4 May under the direction of the TUC General Council. The union executives were asked to confirm that they would place their powers in the hands of the TUC General Council for the purpose of the strike.

Wills was out of London – in Devon – and did not take part in the TUC conference of union Executives. But the president, W. Loveland, and two members of the EC, I. Stokes and W. Stevens, had represented the NUCW at the conference and on Sunday 2 May they reported back to an emergency meeting of the EC. A resolution was adopted which declared the willingness of the EC to put the whole of the NUCW's resources at the disposal of the TUC General council and to abide by its instructions; a letter to this effect was then sent to Walter Citrine, the TUC acting general secretary. By the time Wills returned from Devon on the evening of the following day every branch of the NUCW had been sent a telegram instructing members to await instructions from head office before taking strike action. This was followed by a circular which set out the

An East London street scene during the General Strike, 1926

details of the arrangements made by the TUC and gave the following firm instructions:

> All members engaged in Passenger and Commercial Transport must cease work at once. All members employed in the Building Trade must cease work at once, except those employed in House Building and Hospitals, etc. No member employed in Gas and Electricity are to cease work until further orders from this office.

As the General Strike gathered momentum other NUCW members were called out following instructions from the TUC. On 5 May members engaged on road maintenance and repair were instructed to cease work and on 7 May members in electricity supply were called out, where no local agreement had been reached to cut off supplies to industry and commerce while maintaining services to domestic users, health and social services and similar undertakings. But the situation was confused; sometimes NUCW members responded to local committees rather than the union's head office; at other times Wills had great difficulty in getting clear instructions from the TUC General Council; and often there were delays in messages. At one point Wills and Stokes visited the TUC headquarters to try to clear up confusion that had arisen over the position of workers in the power stations. Wills also wrote to the TUC complaining that the exclusion of the NUCW from the advisory committee that had been set up to deal with the public services was causing problems. But at local level there was a widespread feeling of determination and this was often coupled with pressure to step up the pace of the strike. The local strike committee in the London borough of Deptford, for example, urged the TUC to call out the municipal workers so that, in the words of the local strike bulletin, 'the voluntary workers should do the dirty work as well as the clean ... Volunteer strike breakers would be ideally employed in dust collecting and in the sewers, especially the sewers'.[15]

But unknown to the NUCW Executive and almost every other trade unionist in the country a small group of TUC leaders had made the opening moves towards ending the strike only three days after it had started. On 7 May the Special Industrial Committee of the TUC General Council met for talks with Sir Herbert Samuel, Liberal, one-time

Home Secretary and chairman of the Royal Commission on the coal industry that had been set up by the government in 1925. The meeting place was not without significance; it was in the home of Sir Abe Bailey, a South African millionaire and a friend of the railwaymen's leader J.H. Thomas, who was also a Labour MP and a prominent members of the TUC General Council. On the day after meeting the TUC leaders Samuel met representatives of both the coalowners and the government. Thus began a series of exchanges involving the TUC Special Industrial Committee, Samuel and the government which culminated at noon on 12 May when members of the TUC General Council visited 10 Downing Street to tell the Prime Minister, Stanley Baldwin, that they were calling an end to the strike.

The miners' leaders, who had not directly participated in any of the meetings with Samuel, strongly opposed the way in which the TUC General Council was ending the strike; but they were told that through the decision taken at the conference of union Executives on 1 May, the direction of the strike was in the hands of the TUC General Council – and it had decided to end the strike. The miners therefore remained in dispute, locked out by the coalowners until they were forced back to work by defeat six months later.

The first indication that the NUCW had that the General Strike had been called to an end was a telephone call from the TUC to Wills in the afternoon of 12 May which was followed, a few hours later, by a telegram reading: 'General Council Trades Union Congress have today declared general strike terminated. Please instruct your members as to resuming work as soon as arrangement can be made. Letter follows.' Wills then despatched telegrams to all NUCW branches: 'Strike over; all men to return to work at once'. Outside the TUC General Council and the leaders of the Mineworkers' Federation, few trade unionists had any notion that events had developed to this point and at first there was a shocked sense of disbelief; this was followed by anger that the TUC leaders had left the miners to fight alone in circumstances which undermined the strength of the whole trade union movement.

The main thrust of the strike, which was still not fully extended when the TUC terminated the action, had been in transport and the manufacturing industries, according to the plan approved by the conference of union executives; thus at no stage had the majority of NUCW members been involved. But in a number of areas there were strong concentrations of NUCW members amongst the workers called out; in Edinburgh, for example, members in the electricity supply walked out along with 400 engaged in road works.[16] In some places members employed in public health departments stopped work, against TUC instructions, as they were caught up in the momentum of the strike. An indication of the degree of the involvement of NUCW members was the payment of £2,833 in dispute benefit; this expenditure plus a donation of £1,800 to the Miners' Federation (of which almost £1,000 was raised by a levy on the members) pushed NUCW finances almost £1,500 into the red in 1926. One of the small, and as yet unsolved, puzzles of the Corporation Workers' involvement in the General Strike is how it came to have a dozen members who were miners and who, as delegates to the 1927 conference were told, remained locked out – and presumably drawing dispute pay – until November.

Finance, however, was only a minor problem for the NUCW in the wake of the General Strike. Much more important was the need for it to confront the difficulties created for the trade unions by the government which, building on its victory in the General Strike, introduced new legislation to further weaken an already demoralised trade union movement. The 1927 Trade Disputes and Trade Unions Act was wide ranging in its application; it made a general strike and most sympathetic strikes illegal, imposed harsh restrictions on picketing, forced civil service unions to leave the TUC, and by altering the way in which the political levy operated severely weakened the finances of the Labour Party. For the NUCW and other unions organising workers employed by public authorities, the Act created an additional problem; it prohibited local and other public authorities from making trade union membership a condition of employment and prohibited public bodies from including union membership clauses in contracts made with private contractors. The Act also exposed thousands of workers in the public services to prosecution for criminal breach of contract if they failed to provide services through taking strike action. When the

NUCW's national conference met at Exeter in June 1926, the new law, which was then on its way through parliament, figured prominently in the presidential address by J.T. Bailey. He told delegates that the object of the legislation, 'the Blacklegs' Charter' he called it, was to turn the clock back to the time when men were sent to penal servitude 'for exhibiting Trade Union Spirit'. And he warned that it contained

> grave dangers to our freedoms and privileges as municipal employees ... The legal status of Trade Unions will be entirely altered and careful consideration will have to be given to our policy and our administration if we are not to be landed in legal difficulties ... The Executive Committees are to be the gaol-birds and criminals of the future.

In one respect the NUCW was better placed than many other unions, as Bailey noted when he told delegates to the 1927 conference: 'We are pleased to say that we have been able to maintain our financial membership unimpaired.' The experience of some other unions was very different; the economic depression and its consequent unemployment had reduced union membership from more than 8,000,000 in 1920 to 5,500,000 by 1925 and by the year after the General Strike the TUC affiliated membership had slumped to 3,800,000. One of the advantages enjoyed by municipal workers in times of economic depression was continuity of employment, and as job losses were not as high as in manufacturing industry the NUCW was not badly affected by membership losses – as evidenced by the fact that its membership remained fairly steady at around 12,000 throughout the mid-1920s. But despite its stable membership the strength of the NUCW was still heavily concentrated in relatively few geographical areas, which made it vulnerable to local upsets. In Bermondsey, where Wills lived and the head office was situated, three branches accounted for almost 1,000 members while another London branch, LCC Parks, had 800 members.

By far the biggest branch was in Edinburgh, which by 1926 had reached a total of almost 2,000 members; so when difficulties began to upset the functioning of the branch the EC was forced to take action. After examining the problems the EC decided, in October 1927, that they centred around the full-time organiser Carabine who – according to the EC – had 'not obeyed the instructions of this Council'. The Executive took the drastic step of giving Carabine a month's notice to terminate his employment and then re-engaged him on a six month probationary period. At the same time the EC questioned the high level of branch expenditure and ordered that a more prudent financial policy be adopted. The situation did not improve and in March 1928 the EC expressed disquiet over the lack of progress in implementing its plans for the branch. The following months Carabine, who had been off sick for a time during his probationary period, resigned on the grounds of ill health and the EC was faced with the need to appoint a new organiser to give urgent attention to a branch which accounted for one-sixth of the union's entire membership. In May, Jack Airlie, a boilermaker and an Independent Labour Party member of the Edinburgh council, was appointed by the EC to reorganise and revitalise the most important branch of the union.

In addition to its internal problems with the Edinburgh branch, the NUCW also had external difficulties in Scotland. They arose when the Electrical Trades Union took strong objection to the organisation by the Corporation Workers of electricity supply workers who were employed by Edinburgh council. The conflict between the two unions culminated in the exclusion of the NUCW from the JIC for the electricity industry, an exclusion which the NUCW was unable to reverse. There was also conflict with the ETU in the Corporation Workers' other centre of strength: Bermondsey. The problems originated in 1925 when a member of the ETU objected to working alongside a wireman's mate who had been transferred from another department and who was a member of the NUCW. This led to a strike of ETU members in Bermondsey and Hackney which was eventually resolved but which left a legacy of bitterness amongst some members of the ETU (others had opposed the strike).[17]

In February 1927 the trouble at Bermondsey flared up again when 37 ETU members walked out on strike because the NUCW – at the request of the council which operated a closed-shop policy – admitted into temporary membership a wireman's mate while he was awaiting clearance of his application for ETU membership. As part of its efforts to end the dispute the NUCW offered to transfer the man to the ETU but the offer was refused and the strike only ended when, after three weeks, the matter was referred to the TUC Disputes Committee. In its findings the Disputes Committee, while criticising the NUCW for accepting the man into membership while a dispute was in progress, commended it for offering to transfer him to the ETU and concluded, 'the position need not have arisen had the ETU acted in a more reasonable manner'. On the major claim by the ETU, that it should be recognised as having a monopoly on membership in the installation department of the Bermondsey Council, the Disputes Committee said:

> We cannot express any opinion, as the consideration of such a claim does not come within the Standing Orders governing the hearing of disputes, and previous decisions of Congress have already laid it down that the General Council cannot admit the claim of any Union to an exclusive right to organise in any section of industry.

The NUCW considered that the TUC Disputes Committee report was a vindication of its attitude. In a lengthy report on the affair, Wills said that the quarrel was not between the ETU and the NUCW but between the ETU and 'all other unions catering for municipal employees'. Warning the ETU that its policies would force councils into acting against the general interests of trade unionism, Wills concluded his report by asking: 'What more can a Council do than to insist upon all employees belongong to a Union, and leave it to the employees and the unions as to which union a man shall belong?'[18]

In effect, Wills was restating his belief in industrial unionism but at the same time indicating that the NUCW was prepared to reach accommodation with other unions in making working agreements. In this he differed from his predecessor Albin Taylor and this was even more markedly demonstrated when, early in 1928, Wills and Ernest Bevin – on behalf of the NUCW and the TGWU – concluded a working agreement under which the Corporation Workers relinquished any claims to organise uniformed staff in the tram and bus services. There was some disagreement over this move from active NUCW members in the tramway services who argued that they had not been consulted; but Wills considered it important to establish the NUCW's position in the trade union movement by this kind of agreement and he told the 1928 TUC that the Corporation Workers would be prepared to consider similar agreements with other unions. It was an offer which received no response.

At the same time as he was endeavouring to consolidate and extend the union's position in the trade union movement, Wills was anxious to introduce changes in the union's internal organisation and administration. He wanted it to be better equipped to service its members and to respond to members' interests by extending participation in the structure of decision making. For example, in October 1927 he floated the idea that district committees, composed of branch officials and lay members, would provide a forum for discussion on common problems, particularly in relation to JICs, and would provide a link between the branches and the EC. It was not surprising – given the location of Wills's office, home and council activities – that these ideas were taken on board in London and that the first district committee was established there a few months after he had suggested the possibility.

Another move to improve the union's efficiency was to acquire a new head office. When the office had been transferred from East Ham to Bermondsey following the appointment of Wills, the EC had made it clear that the move was temporary and that efforts would be made to obtain more suitable permanent accommodation. A sub-committee was set up to find the new office and after an eighteen month search it located a large Victorian House in Aberdeen Terrace, Blackheath – a smart South East London suburb – for £1,800 freehold. It was, as union president J.T. Bailey explained to the 1927 national conference, a valuable investment for the union. Taking into account the loss of interest on the money used to purchase the building and the payment of rates, taxes and maintenance the total cost of the new building would be approximately £1 15s a week against the £1 rent paid for only two rooms in Bermondsey. Into the new offices moved Jack Wills and his secretary Flo Fancett – who played an important role in the union – together with organiser Joe Burgess and a small clerical staff. They were later joined by two other full-time organisers who were initially employed on a temporary basis: Arthur Moyle and George Catchpole, both Labour Party activists in Bermondsey and as such personally well-known to Wills.

Within a few weeks of their appointment Moyle and Catchpole were introduced by the union's president, W. Stevens, to a meeting of delegates from 52 branches at what was to become an occasion of historic significance for the union. It was a special conference called by the EC to consider the possibility of altering the name of the union.

Wills opened the discussion by saying that from time to time branches and members had suggested that the title of the union should be changed to one which would embrace all workers employed in local government service. These suggestions had been given a new sense of immediacy when the Minister of Health had announced that he intended to introduce a Bill to the autumn session of parliament with the object of reforming the machinery of local government. As a result, explained Wills, 'the question of changing the name of the Union became both necessary and urgent'. Of particular concern was the possibility that some of the government's proposals, especially in the field of Poor Law administration, would bring important changes in the position of workers which would require effective union action. Wills explained that when the Bill became law it would extend the influence of rural, urban and county councils over wages and conditions, and 'the outlook of those bodies were dominated entirely by the conditions of the Agricultural Labourer'. In their entirety the changes proposed by the Bill created the need for the union to approach the problem of organisation 'from an entirely different angle', said Wills; and the first step was to change the name of the union 'to make it more embrasive'. Two executive members, Sharp and Loveland, then moved on behalf of the EC an amendment to the rules to delete the words 'National Union of Corporation Workers' from the rule book and substitute 'National Union of Public Employees'. After the defeat of an attempt by the Edinburgh and Pontefract branches to include words 'Corporation Workers' alongside 'Public Employees' in the new title, the president put the EC amendment to the vote and it was carried by 248 votes to nil.

Thus, in the Shaftesbury Hotel, St Martin's Lane, London,

on the morning of Sunday, 19 August 1928, the National Union of Public Employees was born, with forty years of history enabling it to step into the future with confident determination.

NOTES

1. See R. Postgate, *The Builders' History*, London 1923, p. 422; R. Holton, op. cit., pp.67, 144; P. Latham, 'Rank and File Movements in Building, 1910-1920', *Our History*, No.69.
2. *Bermondsey Labour News*, No.21, December 1921.
3. *Daily Mail*, 13 January 1926.
4. N. Branson, *Poplarism 1919-25*, London 1979.
5. *Municipal Journal*, 30 October 1925.
6. Annual Report of TUC 1926. Although the NUCW Resolution was seconded by the TGWU, tensions existed between the Labour Councils and some of the trade union leaders over matters of labour policy and this surfaced in the seconder's speech. Ernest Bevin, TGWU general secretary, felt strongly that in some cases the Councils had made improvements without consulting the unions: 'If the Labour Councils do not conform to this procedure, a very awkward position will undoubtedly be created some time in the future, and the trade unions will be called upon to defend things for which they are in no way responsible'.
   Executive Report to the London Labour Party, 1925/6. See also H. Morrison, *An Autobiography*, London 1966, p.89.
7. *Municipal Journal*, 30 December 1927.
8. Quoted in Woolwich Borough Council Minutes, 27 July 1927.
9. *The Straight Left*, No.1, February 1928.
10. *Bermondsey Labour Magazine*, 27 July 1927. See also the Executive Report to the London Labour Party, 1926/7 and *Southwark and Bermondsey Recorder*, 8 July 1927.
11. Wandsworth Borough Council Minutes, 1 May, 24 July 1923; Finsbury Borough Council Minutes 7 July 1925.
12. *Tottenham and Edmonton Weekly Herald*, 25 April, 25 May 1923.
13. *Finsbury Star*, October 1925.
14. *Municipal Journal*, 17 April 1925.
15. Deptford Official Strike Bulletin, 7 May 1926.
16. Official Strike Bulletin of Edinburgh and District Strike Committee, Nos 1 and 8.
17. *Southward and Bermondsey Recorder*, 3 July, 10 July 1925; Hackney Borough Council Electricity Committee Minutes, 23 September 1925.
18. *A Record of the Facts in connection with the Dispute between the ETU and the Bermondsey Borough Council*, NUCW, 1927.

A Note on Sources

Very little survives in the form of official union archives for the years covered by this volume. The disappearance of an entire union organisation, secessions, splits and office moves have left gaping holes in the available records.

For years it was believed that NUPE's precursor, the London County Council Employees' Protection Association was formed almost single-handedly by Albin Taylor in 1888. This and other elementary mistakes – particularly about the early years – were first made at the time of Taylor's death in an obituary writters in 1936. Most of Taylor's contemporaries from the 1890s had either moved on or passed away and the available records – miscellaneous and disparate – didn't help. So a version of union history was created which seemed reasonable and which was repeated uncorrected in union publications – and even some general trade union histories – for the next fifty years. The notable exceptions to this were Clegg, Fox and Thompson's meticulous *History of British Trade Unions Since 1889*, and Clegg's own history of the GMWU where the chronology of the early organisations was correctly stated.

This volume of official history is based on a piecing-together of evidence and hopes to set the record straight. In attempting to construct a picture of early municipal workers' trade unionism it has been necessary to use a wide variety of sources, a flavour of which can be gained from the footnotes at the end of each chapter. Where official union archive material is quoted it is not accompanied by a reference as the source is either stated or obvious. The location of these and other useful records and primary sources are listed below in a selected guide.

A. COLLECTIONS OF HISTORICAL MATERIAL

At the Modern Records Centre (NUPE Archive):

West Ham National Municipal Incorporated Vestry Employees' Labour Union Minute Books, 1892-1900.
Papers relating to Municipal Employees' Association dispute 1906-7.
National Union of Corporation Workers:
  Quarterly Report, 1907-1913
  Report and Balance Sheet, 1916, 1919, 1920
  Executive Council Minutes, 1918-1928
  Report of Annual Conference, 1912-1928
  Miscellaneous papers
National Joint Industrial Council (Non-Trading) Minutes from 1919.
Various Regional Joint Industrial Council Minutes from 1920.

At the GMBATU National College, Manchester:

Municipal Employees' Association Executive Council Minutes, 1900-7.
National Union of Gas Workers and General Labourers Reports from 1889.

At Congress House:

Municipal Employees' Association Annual Reports, 1901-2.
Quarterly Journal and Reports, 1903-6.
TUC Disputes Committee Minutes.

At the Greater London Records Office:

Proceedings on the London County Council and Minutes and Presented Papers of Committees from 1889.
LCC Salaries and Wages Books, 1890-1900.
Metropolitan Water Board Minutes from 1902.

At the National Museum of Labour History:

National Municipal Labour Union Minutes and Papers, 1898-1900.
Canning Town Social Democratic Federation Minute Book, 1890-1893.
Canning Town Gas Workers' Union Minute Book, 1891-3.

At Labour Party Head Office:

Labour Representation Committee and Labour Party Papers from 1900.

At Herbert Morrison House:

London Labour Party Minutes from 1919.

At the British Library:

Burns Collection of diaries and correspondence.

At the British Library of Political and Economic Science:

Webb Trade Union Collection.
Booth Collection.
London Trades Council Minutes and Annual Reports.

At the Public Records Office:

Files of the Registrar of Friendly Societies of registered trade unions.
Files of the Industrial Commissioner.

B. MUNICIPAL RECORDS

Minutes of London Vestries, Borough and Town Councils referred to in the footnotes are kept normally by the local history section of the respective modern local authority public library.

Index